Margaret Kane

THEOLOGY
IN AN INDUSTRIAL
SOCIETY

SCM PRESS LTD

334 01630 4
First published 1975
by SCM Press Ltd
56 Bloomsbury Street, London

© SCM Press Ltd 1975

Printed in Great Britain by
Northumberland Press Limited
Gateshead

CONTENTS

I

BEGINNING WHERE WE ARE

Technology and industry are shaping the lives of us all. This is just as true for those who do not work in industry or live in an industrial area as for those who do. The whole of our society is influenced by what happens in industry, and it is in industry that the struggle for meaning is most sharply focussed. The huge towers and columns of the chemical and steel works, the cranes and winding gear of shipyards and pits not only indicate where men are to work and live, but also raise questions about the meaning of life and the meaning of faith.

Is man simply a cog in the whole process? If he was sucked into the technological process in its early stages, is he now to be discarded as technology progresses? Has technology taken on a life of its own to which man's own life must be subservient? Or can man use technology for his own ends? And if man is able to choose, what exactly are the ends that he should pursue? What is the meaning of it all? How is man to understand his own life within our industrial world? What faith can enable him to respond and live as a complete and responsible human being?

These questions are at the heart of the search for meaning in life and in faith. They also show that we are not involved in two separate searches, one for life and one for faith, but in one exploration that seeks the meaning of both life and faith together. Too often life and faith have been separated, so that faith has seemed irrelevant to life, and the human struggle has seemed of secondary importance in the search for meaning in faith. As a result both life and faith have become meaningless.

This book is about the one search for meaning in life and in faith. It starts from the belief that we must take industrial society absolutely seriously, and that we must take theology equally seriously. Theology in this book is not seen as something that can be done by theologians in isolation from everything else, but as something that must be done in and for an industrial society, and in relation to everything else. The book suggests how this may be done and describes how it is actually being done now.

If we want to know something about a person one of the first questions we ask is what his job is. If we know that he is a boilermaker, a miner, a clerk, a doctor, or a bank manager, we feel we have a clue to understanding the person himself. A person's work cannot be seen simply as a part of his life, for it colours his whole life and in some sense it has made him what he is.

In industrial society, the older forms of community, which had a certain unity about them have been destroyed so that in our present society people are divided into different groupings each of which has its own background, outlook and aspirations. For instance managers and trade unionists represent two different communities which are divided in many ways by different interests. What your job is determines where you live, who you mix with, what you do in your spare time and how you understand the meaning of life. It shapes your own future and the future of your children.

But this future is very uncertain, for the relative continuity and stability of pre-industrial society has given way to changes which follow each other with increasingly rapid and disruptive effects. This is the kind of power technology has over us, and why we must take industrial society absolutely seriously.

There are of course some people for whom this is not obvious. They would like to ignore the whole business – and they may do so until a break-down in one of the essential services, or some financial measure forces them to see that industry is also important to *them*. Then there is no escape from the fact that we are all in it together and that we must all be concerned with the search for meaning in our industrial society.

What may have been helpful in the past becomes an irritating strait-jacket for today, so that new efforts have to be made to pursue the search, for the changes that technology and industry bring about break up any temporary solutions that may have been reached.

This search must start where we are. It is *this* life we must make sense of, and it is with *our* concerns that we must start if Christian faith is to mean anything to us at all.

Theology, the search for meaning, is not something for the 'chosen few' who happen to be 'that way inclined', but for all of us, for we all have to struggle to find meaning in life and meaning in faith. The struggle always takes place in specific situations and in relation to particular people and events.

This book is based on experience which I have shared with others in the struggle for meaning. The context is the North East of England, where there is no need to remind people of the importance of technology and industry, for it is a prime example of how the life of a whole region is shaped and re-shaped by technological and industrial change. The main factors in the history of the area are the three rivers – the Tyne, the Wear and the Tees, and the rich deposits of coal in County Durham and parts of Northumberland. North Sea oil and gas have not yet made their full impact but serve to show how change of one kind or another follows technological patterns. Change opens up new possibilities, but it can also be a threat to the security and identity of many people. If security has depended on learning a trade, what happens when this skill is no longer needed? What does it mean for a mining community when their pit closes down? Will there be jobs for young people if they stay longer at school? These questions concern people and it is with people that I am concerned.

The church's concern is also with people and their needs, but the changes of technology and industry have raised problems for its traditional ways of ministry, and so the church must also change.

The churches in the North East are changing in a number of ways. There is more co-operation between the denominations, team ministries have been established and some ministers have been appointed to relate to particular aspects of the life of society such as industry. All these changes may be of some use to the church itself in its internal efficiency, but they hardly touch the real needs of the world. For that to happen a fundamental theological change is needed. It was the urgency of this need that made the appointment of a theological consultant necessary.

My appointment in 1969 to the post of theological consultant in the North East was a new departure and was made so that I might help the churches engage with people throughout the North East in the search for meaning in life and in faith.

I was appointed by the Bishop of Durham in consultation with church leaders ecumenically to work in the region that includes Northumberland, Durham and the part of North Yorkshire that is included in Teesside.[1]

Before that I had been working to overcome the divorce between life and faith in a series of different situations – first in a mining parish in South Yorkshire, then working with steel workers and coal miners as a chaplain of the Sheffield Industrial Mission and finally in a short term appointment to start industrial mission work in Hong Kong for the Hong Kong Christian Council. It was only because of this extensive experience that I was able to undertake the theological task that lies at the heart of the search for meaning.

In the mining parish I came to understand the dominance of industry over every aspect of life in a personal way, for I had digs in a home where the father and one son worked at the pit and a younger son was still at school. All three had different shifts, so there was seldom a time when it was not necessary to keep quiet while one of them was sleeping.

In the steel works in Sheffield another aspect of the effect of industry upon life prompted a question that summed up many people's experience: 'Must life always be a matter of man against man, or is genuine concern for others a possibility?'

Hong Kong is about as far from Sheffield as you can get, but it was because I had worked in the steel works of Sheffield that I was invited to work with the textile, garment and other workers in Hong Kong. The questions of meaning that emerge in this rapidly developing economy are the same as those in other industrial societies – so that Hong Kong can also teach us a lot.

This book describes some of the issues that have emerged from my work as a theological consultant in the North East region and gives some clues about the direction for the continuing struggle to find meaning in life and faith. Because it is concerned with the meaning of God's action within life today, it is a theological book. I am aware that misunderstandings about theology are so great that this statement raises problems and an attempt is made to meet these questions in the course of the book.

I must emphasize the fact that my concern is first and foremost with the struggle for meaning in life and not with the survival or role of the church. Of course we must consider how the church and how the individual Christians can share more effectively in this struggle, but if this is our main concern, everything else will be distorted. The Christian gospel is not about self-concern but freedom from self for the service of others.

What I want to share is an experience of wrestling with others in an industrial society to find meaning in life and faith. Because I am also involved in the search I have only been able to catch a glimpse of meaning and wholeness, but this is enough to make me realize that there is meaning beyond anything I can grapple with yet. So the book does not suggest a completed search but offers an invitation to share in a continuing search.

If Christian faith is to mean anything to us we must start where we are and with our concerns. This is why I am starting where I am – in the North East of England and with the concerns of the people of the North East. That concern is with people and their lives and that is why I am starting with four actual people and with their concerns as they described them in a quite ordinary conversation. Because technology and industry are so central to all our lives I am starting with the conversation of four men who all work in industry.

'I am doing all I can to keep the jobs of people in this town and if possible to find more jobs.' The speaker, Bob, is a trade union convenor in an engineering works in Hartlepool. His factory is part of a firm which has a number of plants in different parts of the North East. In his own plant there has been a constant change of management which has made open relationships difficult. 'How can you work constructively with managers who are here for such a short time that they are totally uncommitted to the firm and to the people in it?' Bob asks. This is a major question for him, for without warning it has been announced that the majority of the workers in his factory are to be made redundant and many of the machines moved to another factory in the region. 'The main problem is lack of trust throughout industry,' he concludes.

'Managers must be as ruthless as the system in which they have to work,' replies John, who is a manager in the British Steel Corporation's Hartlepool works. 'Senior managers are under pressure. This leads them to put pressure on their subordinates, and so on all the way down the line.'

'But our firm is also a part of the British Steel Corporation and we find relationships between management and men are extremely good.' This comment was made almost in chorus by the other two members of the group, a manager and a steel worker from Consett Iron Works. It seems that the comparative remoteness of their situation in West Durham has made them less affected by change than the others, but in fact, their insistence on the outstandingly good relationships in their firm could be a measure of their underlying anxiety about what steel nationalization may eventually mean for Consett.

As a local councillor Bob has for some time been deeply concerned with the high unemployment in Hartlepool. When the threat came to close his own firm, he was determined to save it, and called a mass meeting of all employees from whom he gained backing for action to stop the machines being moved. This step was followed by an intensive search for new orders, during which Bob wrote many letters and visited key people throughout the country.

He is the man in the middle of a situation which is not a straightforward black and white issue between management and trade unions, for there are considerable tensions between the two unions Bob has to represent as convenor. Even among his own members there is a tendency not to care about those who are made redundant so long as the rest can get extra overtime earnings. This leaves Bob very much alone with a burden of concern and responsibility for others which few people are ready to share.

As a manager, John has his own burdens. Since nationalization, steel has been going through a series of changes. It has not been an easy time for anyone in the industry and, with the announcement of plans for the new steel complex on the south bank of the Tees, it is likely that the Hartlepool plant will be run down. John's main energies have been taken up with his work. He occasionally has a few drinks with work acquaintances and goes to meetings of his professional association, but otherwise he tries to keep a clear separation between work and private life. Perhaps it is because he feels the pressure of his work situation upon him to become a certain type of person who is single minded in pursuit of industrial efficiency, that he tries to protect at least one part of his life and personality from this all-consuming demand.

Consett, where Jonathan and Fergus live and work is situated in the West Durham countryside, well away from the urban areas. The Consett Iron Company employs 6,500 men. Since most of the coal mines in the area are now closed, the Iron Company is the main employer, not only for Consett, but for the surrounding area. Recently some modern firms have moved into Consett, but they employ comparatively few workers and the continued existence of Consett as a community still depends largely on the iron works. In contrast with Bob's activities in Hartlepool, neither Jonathan nor Fergus are particularly active in local affairs. Their interests are more domestic for both are keen gardeners and enjoy the countryside.

This is simply a conversation between four men, but they are typical of many others, and we have started with an industrial example because it is industry that has shaped and is shaping our world. It is clear that these men's work cannot be seen simply as a part of their lives but that it has an influence on every part of their lives, so that we have good reason to speak of an industrial society. We can also see in this conversation that managers and trade unionists approach their common questions from different points of view.

This underlines the fact that we must take industrial society absolutely seriously and why it is so urgent for theology to be done, in and for an industrial society.

This group's comments about the church are also typical and can help us to see something of the divorce in most people's minds between Christian faith and the real concerns of their lives.

Bob lives in a council house and his concern for others is just as evident in his home life as at work. He has six children, some of whom are married. What with children's friends, and grandchildren, it is not always easy to know who's who in a home where there is always time and space for anyone in need. He lives practically next door to the parish church, but that is as far as the matter goes. As Bob says, 'It is a pity I don't know the clergy as we are all concerned with the people on this estate.'

'Management cannot afford to be soft and therefore Christianity and work cannot mix,' says John, who sees Christianity as belonging to the domestic side of life. He has always lived in the Hartlepool area and was brought up in the Congregational Church, but has had no active connection with it since he was eighteen years old. His children go to the local Church of England church and John has become involved in the scout parents' association, helping with their efforts to raise money for camping equipment and so on.

Jonathan was brought up nominally Church of England and Fergus, Methodist but neither of them attend their churches now.

It is clear that none of these men have been helped by the little contact they have had with the church, to understand the ultimate questions of life as they experience it.

One factor about this particular group is not typical and that is that each one of them is in contact with an industrial chaplain and their remarks about the chaplain's presence in their firms are illuminating.

'The chaplain had a rough time when he attended a Works' Council meeting in convincing some of the members that he could offer a service to industry, but in the end there was only one dissenter,' said Bob.

'The church is trying to bring the church to the people and to meet them on their own ground, and the majority like it,' said Fergus. 'The effect is to start men thinking that the church is trying to do something.'

'They are educating themselves on the needs of the people to know what living is,' said Jonathan. 'The chaplains we know can mix with people and they encourage creative action by advising people in an unobtrusive manner.'

'We have discussed industrial development, government policy on retraining and had visits to other factories, but the one subject we have never talked about is religion,' said John. 'There is no obtrusion of theological expertise, but without forcing the church on people they can see that it is there. Not every cleric could do this and above all a chaplain must not be introduced as a "Bible puncher" or he is on a dead wicket from the start.'

'The main achievement of the chaplain is that he helps people to trust each other,' said Bob. 'One effect is that I now look forward to sitting down with management in a management/ trade union group run by industrial mission. I have learnt to respect the attitudes and opinions of the other side. People live separate lives and industrial mission can bring them face to face without being in a negotiating situation. In this way you get to know people as they are. But of course only the fringes of the job have been touched so far.'

What they say about the chaplains shows that these men do not fully understand what the chaplains are trying to do, but that all the same something is happening to bridge the gap between the main concerns of people's lives and Christian faith. Because the chaplain had come to meet them on their own ground and shown that he was concerned with their affairs, they were beginning to realize for the first time that Christian faith is to do with life. Their previous experience of the church and of Christians had suggested just the opposite. No wonder that their expectations about the sort of things a clergyman might do had made them unable either to see or express exactly what the chaplain was doing.

Every chaplain has to deal with false expectations before he starts regular visiting in a works, and has to allay fears that he may simply be aiming at getting people to church, forcing religion down their throats or on the other hand using his position to interfere with the proper responsibilities of management or trade unions.

But we are all in the search together and the chaplain himself has a problem about his own role, for as soon as he admits that the search for meaning in life and for meaning in faith is one and the same, he must begin to question his own role and as he asks whether there is any meaning in life he must also ask whether there is any meaning in faith. This was the question that faced the German theologian Bonhoeffer, who for many years had worked as a theologian in his church, but when he was imprisoned by the Nazis he had to face the question of meaninglessness in life in a more radical way. He saw then that 'the foundation is taken away from the whole of what has up to now been our "Christianity",' and it is necessary to ask afresh 'What Christianity really is, or indeed who Christ really is for us today.'[2]

But this is what theology is about – it is about facing life as a whole, doing this as a whole person and doing it in hope. Those who have the courage to do this reject the way of palliatives and commit themselves to a continuing search for wholeness and meaning.

In this sense the chaplain simply aims to be a representative of what it is to be a Christian and to have faith. This faith is that God is already active in the situation and that in and through the concrete happenings and events of life he is offering himself in love to men, who are called to respond within the day to day framework of their own lives. What is needed is that people should become open to this reality and should respond even though they may not see the full meaning of what they are doing, and even though they may not think of God or mention his name. What this means for those of us who are concerned with the Christian mission is that we must take the world including industry seriously for itself and not as a means to something else. We must try to understand it and to be discerning about what is happening in the light of our understanding of the meaning of life and of faith.

What this means in terms of action will depend on the situation. In the particular conversation I have recorded one problem that is identified is the divisions that exist between the various groups in industry. What is needed is that the people concerned should be helped to relate to each other across these divisions, so that they can talk and listen to each other. This in itself will not solve all their problems but it will enable them to look at their industrial life together and to identify the causes of the rifts and to see wider scope for their responses.

This may all seem far removed from 'doing theology', which is what this book is about, but I believe this is exactly where we must start if we are to do theology in an industrial society, and I shall now go on to show why I believe theology must start in this way.

NOTES

1. As the work described in this book mainly took place before April 1974, the place names that are used are those that obtained prior to the government reorganization of that year.
2. Dietrich Bonhoeffer, Letters and Papers from Prison, from a letter dated 30 April 1944, SCM Press 1967, pp. 279, 280.

THE VISION

II

REVELATION
God Still Makes Himself Known

God has to be discovered in the situation. It is in and through the people we meet, the day to day happenings of life and the historical events of the world that God comes to us and seeks to make himself known. This is a simple statement but I want to spend some time looking at what it means so that we can give an answer to the question 'How do people come to know God and put their faith in him?' This is at the heart of what this book is about and we shall see that when different answers are given to this question different understandings of the nature of theology and of mission inevitably follow.

That God is known in the day to day things of life is not something I have thought up for myself; it is a faith that has been given to me in and through the people and events of my own life. As it happened I was told a good deal about God, but it was not this that had the greatest influence on me, but meeting with people in and through whom I began to sense that I was also meeting God. In quite ordinary things I became aware of depth and meaning – sitting round a camp fire with a group of youngsters, crowding into an air raid shelter, joking with a young girl who was dying, being sacked from a job, and so on. The common factor seems to be the shattering of complacency and the call to 'wake up'. I have been able to understand this experience as that of someone who comes to me before I look for him by seeing how the Bible and Jesus Christ tell of a God who is always present and always coming to people in love, seeking to make himself known and to call out a response of love.

All people share the same general experiences of life. At some time or another all of us experience love, suffering, wonder and challenge and are lifted out of ourselves in such a way that we

see ordinary things in new ways and sense for a moment a quality
of life of which we are not generally aware.

We each respond to these moments in our own way. Bob for
instance responded to the threatened closure of his factory by a
deep commitment to help those who were in danger of losing
their jobs, but others in the same situation saw this as an opportunity for their own gain. Whatever choice is made it changes
both the situation and the person himself.

This is all a matter of common experience. The difference lies
in the different interpretations that are given to these experiences
and in this Christians have a specific point of view.

Christians believe that it is in day to day happenings and
historical events that men meet God, and have a chance to respond
to and co-operate with him in his purposes. This understanding
means that the realities of the universe and the day to day
meetings and events of life must be taken absolutely seriously.
Christians claim that their insights are not simply a matter of
opinion nor have they been arrived at by common sense, but
that they are the result of God making himself known. It is God
who has taken the initiative to reveal himself, not man who has
discovered God. God has chosen to enter into a personal relationship with man and he has done this by making himself known
to particular people in particular events on particular occasions.
This is what Christians mean by revelation and it is this concept
that we must examine in order to get rid of some misconceptions.

1. The first misconception concerns the nature of knowledge.
Some people think that we know things in a purely objective
way by looking at them from outside. Knowledge of this kind is
something you can possess and hand on to others. On this view
revelation may be seen as God putting propositions into the minds
or individuals from outside, as the result of which they have
information not previously available which they hand on to
others. It is as if the TV mechanic came to install my set and left
a list of instructions about how to adjust it and get different
stations. He would seem to be handing some of his own expertise
to me on a slip of paper. This almost mechanical view of knowledge runs through a lot of thinking about qualifications and
examinations, for instance, as if by going through a certain course
one could accumulate something objective, guaranteed by the
letters after one's name.

The Bible has a different and more profound view of knowledge, which is best represented by the idea of inter-action or
communion. Objects and events are known in a personal way as

we live with them and participate in them. I know the flat I live in, in a way that goes beyond the estate agent's description: I know the last general election in a different way from the way any history book will ever describe it. It is because I have a particular and personal relationship with both. This is not the kind of knowledge that can be handed on in the way the TV mechanic hands me a slip of instructions. The Bible's understanding of knowledge is particularly relevant to our knowledge of people, for we can only know people if they are prepared to make themselves known to us in some way and to give and take in some kind of personal relationship.

It is this personal understanding of knowledge that runs through the Bible. And it is this view of knowledge that lies behind the biblical understanding of revelation. Revelation is not concerned with giving new facts to people, but with the self-giving of God in a relationship with people. Revelation is essentially a self-giving and a communion and it proceeds by dialogue and response. This cannot be handed on mechanically but must be received in a person to person relationship. God makes himself known to people, and people are helped to receive this revelation through and in their relationship with other people.

I am not saying that there are no propositions about God and about faith, but I am saying that faith in God does not come to us from these propositions. The basic fact of Christian faith is the meeting of God and man, and any speaking about God is conditional on this meeting.

This understanding of revelation as a personal encounter rather than as the imparting of propositional information is made in a telling way in the Bible story of Job. Job was a good man, no one had anything against him, he had plenty of money and a nice family. Then he was struck by a devastating series of misfortunes. He lost all his money, his sons and daughters were killed and he himself contracted a crippling and painful disease. Not unnaturally he asked, 'Why should God allow this to happen to me?'

Then his friends came along and they went into all sorts of arguments to explain what had happened to him and why it was all in keeping with God's will. But none of this helped Job at all and he called them a 'windy' lot (Job 16.3). It was only after he had gone through all this agonizing about what it all meant that Job was brought to a point where he was confronted by God himself. This meeting gives him no answer to his question, nor does it give him any information that might help him find an

answer. What it does do is to change Job's whole attitude to life:
'I had heard of thee by the hearing of the ear, but now my eye sees thee; therefore I despise myself and repent in dust and ashes' (Job 42.5-6).

2. As well as showing revelation as a personal meeting, this story illustrates a second point about revelation that is often misunderstood; that is that its positive effect is transformation. If we say negatively that revelation is not primarily about information we can say positively that it is about transformation. Job did not get the answer he was looking for but he was changed and that meant that he was able to go back into the same situation, see it in a new way and respond to it in a new way. God's self-revelation had transformed Job and transformed the situation.

This gives us an enormously important insight into the nature of God's purpose as being concerned with the transformation of the entire universe from within. This insight grows out of the biblical understanding of revelation and must be borne in mind when we consider the nature of mission. For, as I have pointed out already, misunderstanding about mission inevitably follows misunderstandings about revelation, so we face the same danger of an emphasis on propositional statements at the cost of a vision of transformation.

The direct confrontation of God and man is the creative and transforming heart of Christian faith, and this can never be fully articulated or passed on. What ministry and mission must do is to help people and situations become more open and receptive to a transcendence that is in their midst. We shall see in the next chapter that this understanding of revelation gives a new urgency to the intensification and deepening of our theology – and to developing a style of theology that starts at the point where God is making himself known to people today.

3. One further point about revelation may be drawn from the story of Job – that is that what is revealed is never what people expect or could deduce or even what they want to know. 'In the biblical tradition there is a very strong element of unexpectedness, of judgment, of transforming newness.... It is part of and proceeds from, a positive activity of a God positively conceived of.'[1] In the kind of climate when it is often suggested that there is not much difference between one opinion or another it is necessary to underline the fact that the kind of things that Christians are committed to are not simply equivalent to normal common sense.

4. A fourth point about God's self-revelation is that it is always

made through particular people and events. This is a difficult and unacceptable point, but it is in keeping with the essentially personal (but not individualistic) nature of faith. The Jews came to know God as one who they believed was saving them in their experience of escape from Egypt under the leadership of Moses. In this event they also learned something about themselves as they challenged their Egyptian masters and took the risk of a dash to freedom. In the terrifying experience of crossing the Red Sea, they came to a dim awareness of God leading them – an awareness that became more distinct through later experiences and the interpretation of the prophets.

It is in other people and in and through quite ordinary happenings and historical events that God makes himself known.

This sketch of how the Jewish people came to a deeper knowledge of God in the course of their history emphasizes the personal nature of revelation.

God is not absent from any situation but he cannot make himself known unless there is a response and where there is response there is the possibility of further revelation. So the particularity of human history develops in the inter-action of challenge and response, and the process of revelation may be compared to a dialogue in which God speaks and men may either answer or refuse to answer. The dialogue continues according to the kind of response that is made.

5. If we grasp this we shall realize that revelation must be a living continuing process, which in one sense is always new, for each man must meet God for himself in the people and events of his own time and respond within the circumstances of his own life, but in another sense this can only happen if there is a continuing stream of experience within a community, for people are always part of their own community. We are all what we are because we were born into a particular family and brought up with various associations, being influenced in one way or another by their ways of thought and traditions, and we in turn have some influence for good or ill on the communities in which we share. So, although revelation is personal, it is never simply a matter for the individual. The individual is only able to grasp any vision in terms of his own tradition, even though his experience of God may turn his traditions upside down, they are his traditions not someone else's that are being transformed.

We must return to this point when we analyse our present society and consider its various traditions and how individuals contribute new insights within its institutions and groupings.

This is vital to our understanding of what mission means today and of course is essential to any understanding of the church.

We have seen that the Bible shows how particular individuals responded to God's self-revelation and how their response created a community which shared an understanding of God and a relationship with him within which this understanding and relationship could grow, so that out of the same community other individuals could emerge and carry the process a stage further.

Abraham responded to God's urging to leave his country and it was because he responded that the Jewish nation came into being. Moses responded to God's call to suffer with the Hebrew people. The escape from Egypt was believed to have been achieved by God's redemptive activity and the community became bound by a promise and covenant to a deeper relationship with God. From that time prophets, who believed they spoke in God's name and shared God's agony for his people, continually urged men to fulfil their true destiny.

In every case God made himself known in and through particular people, in concrete and particular events and called for response in terms of the concrete situations of the time:

'If you take away from the midst of you the yoke, the pointing of the finger, the speaking wickedness, if you pour out yourself for the hungry and satisfy the desire of the afflicted then shall your light rise in the darkness and your gloom be as the noonday. And the Lord will guide you continually. . . .' (Isa. 58.9-10).

Although it is individuals who receive God's revelation, God's concern is with the whole community and with the individual as a member of his community. And although this process was worked out in a special way in the Jewish people they were asked to recognize that God was not only concerned with them but that his concern with them was in order that they might be concerned with all humanity.

This living process in which the individual response actually forms the community and opens up the possibility of further response should help us to understand why it was only within the Jewish tradition that God was able to make himself known in his fullness.

6. Christians believe that the revelatory process reached its climax and focus in the life, death and resurrection of Jesus. In Jesus people were confronted with the full reality of God and his self-giving love, in Jesus' own life man responds to God completely, and God's purpose is established as the complete self-

giving of God to man and of man to God in an unbroken
communion. In this communion a new quality of life in the Spirit
is begun.

To say that Jesus is the climax of the process points to the fact
that we must see him within the process. Jesus was a Jew and he
shared in the vocation of the Jewish people. The Jewish nation
and its particular vocation emerged from the response that
individuals made to God's self-revelation and their response
shaped the nation and its destiny. Their destiny was to share
God's redemptive love for all men, but for the most part they
had refused to accept God's call. It was left to Jesus to make a
completely self-giving response and he did this by drawing out
and fulfilling the meaning of the fragmentary understanding of
God and his purposes that the Jews had received. In trying to
understand Jesus' place in all this, it is important to hold on to
the two sides of revelation. Christians stress the fact that God
was in Christ revealing himself to men, but it is just as important
to stress Christ as the recipient of revelation:

'The matter of Christ as the recipient or human participant in
revelation is of no small importance. It is in fact the key to the
personal, social and historical character of Christian revelation ...
if revelation is found in the inter-communion of God and man,
then one must look for the highest expression of this covenant
bond and dialogue in the Lord Jesus. He is man receiving as well
as God bestowing; the very meaning of the Incarnation is this
intercourse of divine and human.... In the unique conscious-
ness of this unique individual there takes place fully definitively
the encounter of God and man in redemptive revelation.'[2]

7. I do not think we can understand Jesus' life unless we enter
into something of the mystery of God's tri-unity. Too often we
have a one-dimensional idea of God without any sense of differ-
entiation in his person. If that is so we cannot make sense of the
idea of Jesus responding to God the Father, nor can we grasp
the fact that, as a result of Jesus' unbroken communion with the
Father, he was raised from the dead in the power of the Spirit
and that from that time the Spirit who had always been active in
the world was poured out upon men in a new way.

8. The struggle for meaning in life and for meaning in faith is
one and the same struggle. This is made absolutely clear in the
life of Jesus where God's purpose for man is revealed as that of
achieving full humanity. Jesus does this by making a complete
response in self-giving love to the self-giving love of God. This

sums up what life is about and what it is to be human. It is both means and end – for there is no higher aim than that of communion with God and man, and when this happens it creates an impetus that must transform everything.

What this kind of self-giving response involves is concentrated in the struggle, uncertainty, opposition, failure and renewal that took place in the life, death and resurrection of Jesus Christ. This is not simply an individual struggle, nor is it a struggle in which only Christians are involved; it is the struggle of every man and of all humanity to find meaning in life.

9. A final point must be made about the nature of revelation, and one more misconception removed. A main obstacle to the church's understanding of its mission today is the false idea that because God's self-revealing love is focussed in the life of Jesus of Nazareth that is the end of revelation. The first Christians did not see Christ's resurrection as an end but as a beginning that was to have universal effects. The resurrection was a sign of the beginning of a process that would transform all things – a new creation in which Jesus was 'first born from the dead'. This transformation was not completed all at once but was being brought about by the continued activity of God giving himself through Christ in his Spirit to the world. A true understanding of mission must recognize God's present revelation of himself today in people and events of our time.

In this chapter I have spelt out one view of revelation and what I am going to say in the next chapters depends upon getting this view of revelation clear. But there is another view of revelation and it is important to be clear about what the differences are and to make up our minds where we stand.

This second view sees revelation as mainly concerned with abstract propositions about God that were given to some people but not to others in the past. It understands revelation as objective information that can be handed on from one person to another and from one generation to another.

This is not only different from but opposed to the view of revelation which I have described and which is the source of my own vision and the drive of my own exploring and hope. Revelation in my view is God giving himself so that we may give ourselves. It happens now in the people and events of life, it is a vision about the meaning of life and the meaning of faith, it is about responding to wholeness and doing this as a whole person. This means a transformation now and a concrete possibility here and now. It makes a difference to a present situation, but it is not just that, for it is contact with God and therefore it cannot be planned, nor can we know exactly what we shall discover, but I get occasional glimpses of truth, life and glory. I am only able to grasp any of this in the particular way I do because I am sharing in a search for the meaning of life and faith that involves the whole of humanity.

The contrast between the two views is a contrast between the past and the present, the changeless and the changing, the dead and the living. The differences are so sharp they inevitably lead to different understandings of the nature of theology and the way it should be done, and to different understandings of the nature of mission. It is therefore essential for us to be clear in our understanding of revelation before I go on to speak about theology.

If this chapter has opened up some ideas that you would like to follow up I think that in addition to the books referred to in the notes you would find the following books worth reading:

Gabriel Moran, *God Still Speaks*, Search Press 1967.
T. C. Vriezen, *An Outline of Old Testament Theology*, Blackwell 1966.

NOTES

1. David Jenkins, *What is Man?*, SCM Press 1970, p. 72.
2. Gabriel Moran, *Theology of Revelation*, Search Press 1967, pp. 64, 66.

III

THEOLOGY
The Continuing Search for Meaning in
Life and Faith

This is the densest chapter in the book. It sets out an understanding of what theology is, and of what is involved in shared
theological thinking and exploration, that is 'doing theology'
together. For this reason it may not be an easy chapter to read,
and the following points should be borne in mind:

The whole book is about theology and how it may be done in
an industrial society, and numerous examples of what this means
occur throughout the book. It may therefore be helpful to come
back to this chapter for a second reading after you have read the
whole book.

There is a good deal of 'traditional' language in this chapter –
of course! – because my conviction is that if it were not for the
person of Jesus Christ there would be no theology. In the heart
of the traditions about Jesus Christ there is something unique
that we would not know apart from them.

My complaint is not about Christian 'tradition' as such but
about the separation of faith and life.

There is at present a divorce between life and faith, between
what every person experiences and the work of theologians. But
if it is in the actual people and events of the present that God
is making himself known, theology must consist of reflection
on the meaning of these experiences in the light of the revelation
of God in Christ. In other words it is theology that must unite
the search for meaning in life and faith. If this is to happen we
need a better understanding of what theology is and how it
should be done.

It is present events that force us to ask questions and search
for meaning. Theology must therefore start in the present and is
in principle the concern of every person. This is contrary to the
common view which sees theology as having its beginning and

ending in a study of the Bible and other documents of the past, and of interest only to those who have had special training.

It is this view of theology that is blocking every effort to help people reflect seriously on the meaning of life and faith as one and the same search. Inside and outside the church people are 'turned off' by the mention of theology. For example – a man who over a number of years has initiated a great deal of creative thinking and action in industry, has been led by his experience to a completely changed view of life and recently been confirmed in the Church of England, never loses an opportunity to sneer at any mention of theology.

A church congregation planning their Lent programme and anxious to be active in the community in some way, cannot see that a study of the Bible has any relevance to this activity.

Christian people with a wealth of wisdom and experience cannot see that they have something to contribute to theology, but say 'Leave it to the experts, we are not theologians'.

This attitude runs right through the church where, from top to bottom it is assumed that theology is a matter for a few 'intellectuals' and of no concern to anyone else.

A recent report proposing discussion by the deanery synods on the future of the church in their area said, 'We are less concerned with large issues of church policy and *theology* ... but we are most concerned that the synods be *free* to concentrate on those concerns which directly affect the future of the deanery. . . .' This is typical of many high level church policy statements, which assume that theology is something that inhibits action or that may be brought in after plans have been made and applied to a situation from outside. This attitude ignores the present reality of God in the situation and the ability of people to be aware of his presence and to reflect upon what this means for living. Of course there are reasons for this attitude and the most obvious reason is fear. We all tend to arrange our lives so that we do not have much time to think. We keep on the move and get guilty feelings if we are not busy in one way or another, but the truth is that we are afraid to face ourselves and to face life. We prefer to be at least partially anaesthetized, and only a minority of people reflect deeply upon the meaning of their experience. It is significant that when a group of industrial managers was asked to make a list of theological questions they wanted to consider, one of the first questions was, 'What is the gospel to contented families?'

It seems to me that one of the first things the gospel does is to say, 'Wake up!' You can dare to face the truth, because there is more glory in life than you have yet experienced.

A more serious blockage, however, because it is an unnecessary one, is the style of theology that has moulded our present understanding of theology – some definitions will convey the essence of this type of theology:

'Theology is a subject quite apart....'[1]
'Theology is a body of divinely revealed truths.'[2]
'Theology is the attempt to interpret the documents of revelation and the sacred tradition founded upon them.'[3]
'Theology is the science of thinking about God.'[4]

These definitions suggest that theology is an abstract subject, concerned exclusively with a study of the past and to be left to academic scholars and experts. There is no suggestion that it is in any way concerned with the present life of man, for it clearly relates to a propositional view of revelation.

A second series of definitions shows how different the approach to theology is when revelation is understood as God meeting us in present people and events. It is this style of theology with which we are concerned:

'Theology is a commentary on a contemporary experience of God.'[5]
'Theology which does not correspond with the deepest thoughts and feelings of human beings cannot be a true theology,

' "Ultimately all human problems are theological.... For those who profess to be Christian this means that our deepest concern is with that which is beyond, yet pervasive of, our immediate environment – and the character and nature of that reality is defined in terms of the event of Jesus Christ."[6]

'Unless we see the tremendous difference between these two views of theology we shall not grasp the urgency of the church's theological task. Theology is about finding meaning in life and faith. It is concerned with the question, "What resources do men and women have, and what resources might they have for living hopefully and creatively with the questions which their life in the world puts to their humanity ... ?"

'Now on any Christian assumption theology is relevant to this question because theology is about God, and the centre of the revelation of God in Jesus is what He has done for men, what He will do for us and therefore, what He can now be discovered to be doing for us and how it can be part of our living and hoping.'[7]

This is of concern to every person.

I want to set out quite simply the nature of theology and the theological process as I am beginning to understand it in my own experience:

1. We must begin with the actualities of life and of our own experience. It is this that stirs us and keeps nagging at us so that we have to start questioning and searching, and it is this that has to be wrestled with if we are to find meaning in life and faith. For instance a local councillor was concerned with a question of conflict between the two main political parties on the council and how he could continue to do what he believed to be right without being obsessed with the negative elements of the conflict; a worker wondered about the rights and wrongs of a compromise that had been made when a man flouted union solidarity; a woman supervisor questioned whether it might be she who was in the wrong when people in her section failed to co-operate with each other. These people felt there were questions they wanted to explore, but more often than not reflection has to be stimulated.

2. We must take these actualities seriously. This means paying attention to what is happening in the world, taking the trouble to get our facts right, getting several viewpoints, listening to other people and exploring things in depth. We believe that day to day things matter for their own sake, because it is here that God is active and our job is to discern his action not to introduce something new into the situation. This really takes time – a minister described how he had worked for a whole year with a group in order to understand the meaning of job satisfaction. They had spent most of the year exploring the feelings people had for their jobs, why they had taken these jobs on, or changed from one job to another. It was only when the full human impact of all this had been felt that the group was concerned enough to ask whether there were any resources in Christian faith that might throw light on the question. What happens when proper attention is not given to the mundane realities was brought home forcibly to me when a lecturer in politics, who had done some interesting studies of the civil service spoke to a group. When he realized that it was a Christian group, he expounded his own views on what he considered should be the Christian interest in the subject instead of describing the actual facts of the situation. The result was exhortation not exploration and got us nowhere.

3. We have to look at the actualities of life in the light of God's revelation of himself in Christ. It is this that unifies and

gives meaning to life. This kind of reflection is not simply a
historical enquiry, but an attempt to understand who we are as
Christians, with our own experience of a living Christ, within the
whole stream of Christian experience and witness. Study of the
Bible and what people have made of it is of course an essential
part of this, but if it is isolated from our understanding of our
own destiny, it is dead and meaningless. This is in fact what
Bible study has become for most people. But we must work from
both ends. A purely inductive theology that grows completely
out of the situation is not possible on the view of revelation that
I have accepted. God breaks into a situation with judgment, and
newness that can only be recognized fully in relation to God's
revelation in Christ. So there must be occasions when we study
specific Christian doctrines or parts of the Bible. This point is
often missed when the emphasis on grounding theology in life
is made.

One group I have worked with has found it useful to alternate
the two starting points so that one month they begin with a case
study and the next month with a Christian doctrine.

4. We need to learn from experience of all kinds, and this
means primarily lay experience, we need to listen to others and
to test out our own partial and biased understandings. This
means that we must 'do' theology together. This is where a
complete revolution is needed and especially a revolution in
the role of lay people. At present it is still largely assumed that lay
people will remain passive recipients of sermons and talks given
by clergy. But we need each other's help if we are to find meaning
in life and faith. Christian faith is not meant to be an individualistic and lonely affair but to call us into fellowship ... 'that
which we have seen and heard we proclaim also to you, so that
you may have fellowship with us: and our fellowship is with the
Father and with His Son Jesus Christ' (1 John 1.3).

Everyone has something to contribute to theology from their
own experience. The need to do theology as a joint operation is
obvious when the full cycle of the theological process is understood. There must be a double movement in theology. First
there is an outward movement towards the world and all that is
human, to see all things in the light of Christ. Second there is
an inward movement, with the new conceptual tools and new
information of our own time, for the enrichment and unification
of revelation. These two movements must be in operation if
theology is to be alive. Then the whole of life and the whole of
theology is bringing everything into an organic and intelligible

unity founded on the fullness of revelation in Christ.

5. People outside the church have a vital contribution to make to theology. The fact that theology is concerned with finding meaning in life and faith must make it clear that theology is not simply a matter for church members. In fact church members get trapped in their own internal debates unless they remain open to what is being said by people who look at life from different positions. Because we share a common experience of life we should be able to share our understandings of meaning. This means doing theology in a secular style as something that belongs within a situation not as some formula that is couched in terms derived from another culture and applied to a situation from outside. To do theology in a way that is open to anyone to join in is something that requires skills that have not yet been developed by many Christians.

6. Faith consists in the response of the whole person to the whole of reality. This is expressed first and foremost in living. I have already pointed out that the biblical understanding of knowledge is not of something objective that you possess and can hand on to others, but is a communion and inter-action with people, with life and with God. In the same way truth in the Bible is not something you have and pass on to others by telling them, but is something that has to be lived.

There is a long argument about truth and lies in St John's gospel in which Jesus' opponents try to make out that black is white and to convince themselves that it would be doing God's will to get rid of Jesus. The argument is brought to a head when Jesus says, 'If you continue in my word, you are truly my disciples, and you will know the truth, and the truth will make you free.' Truth here is something to be done, something you live by and something that establishes life.

We all know that we do not discover meaning in life and faith simply by discussion, but by living and exploration.

The word 'integrity' sums up the fact that truth is more than talk. Most people recognize and respect integrity in others and they understand this as a correspondence of word and action.

7. We must express theology in words. None of us can put into words all that we come to know through living experience. But we must struggle to find some way of expressing this if our faith is not simply to be an individualistic matter, but something we share. The words we use are only pointers to the actual realities of life and faith, so we have to use a variety of ways of coming at the same truth if our words are to illuminate rather

than restrict the full meaning. We need to recover a respect for speech as an essential part, though, of course, only a part, of our means of communication with others. This is all part of the reverence for truth that is at the heart of Christian faith.

If we belong fully to the culture of our own time we shall be able to communicate with others in the words and forms that belong to our own time. But we must also make sense of statements of faith from the past that come to us in expressions that are not familiar to our own culture. We must struggle with these statements for they introduce us to the broad stream of Christian experience and help us to gain some understanding of the richness of Christian faith. None of these statements of faith is final but they sum up a good deal of experience gained so far and we, in turn, must make provisional statements, if we are to grasp and go forward from that bit of the truth that we do see.

Christians are among the worst people at communicating even with each other. This springs from an individualism that sees faith as a private matter and attempts to preserve idiosyncrasies of expression at the expense of sharing a common life.

For instance, a group of clergy (about which I will be saying more later) studied the meaning of ministry in a particular town. Their meetings were chaired by a layman. When the clergy were asked to state what they believed the purposes of the church were, it appeared that each one had his own private vision, and that each one was giving the words he used his own special meaning. Only the layman realized the cause of the lack of communication in the group and said, 'You haven't even got an agreed (professional) language with which you can begin to communicate with each other.'

A Council of Churches planned a week-end study for lay members of the churches concerned. Their plan was to work out the content of their faith so that they might engage in evangelistic work. They agreed on a form of words which was in line with the churches' creeds, but when a layman from outside the churches was introduced he could not find any point at which what they were saying was grounded in life experience. The result was that their statements did not convey any meaning to anyone outside their own particular church tradition.

A third example shows how essential it is for any group that is trying to think theologically to keep open to newcomers. In 1970 when I took over a study group that had been meeting for some years, a number of new people joined the group. At the first meeting of the new session one of the original members gave an introductory talk which he had spent a great deal of time preparing. His request for comment at the end of this introduction was greeted by one of the new members exclaiming, 'As clear as mud!' This pitfall is one that any serious theological group can fall into.

The kind of communication that will enable us to think and work together is never easy but it is immensely worthwhile, and the words we use are of course only part of the process.

Although all sorts of people must contribute to theology, academic theologians have a vital role in the process. At present their work is isolated because the church has left them to do theology by themselves. This is precisely what they are not able to do and they need to be brought into serious engagement with thinking that is springing from actual life situations. We need academic theologians but we need to work with them and to use them properly.

There is, however, another kind of theologian that is absolutely crucial to the whole enterprise; that is the theologian who can enable theological thinking to take place throughout the church and in relation to the whole community. This is the kind of job I am committed to and am working on in the North East. This means bringing different groups together, discovering how people of all kinds can work together usefully, identifying various skills in all sorts of people and seeing that these skills are used in the kind of situations where they can develop and serve the whole enterprise. It means making sure that theology does not become an end in itself but bearing in mind that 'the theologian's task is to help the community reach that reflective understanding of Christian truth which is demanded for the full and fruitful living of the Christian life at a particular time'.[8]

This is how I see my job and this book aims to illustrate how I am working this out with others in the various situations of the North East. I have aimed to show in this chapter that theology is for everyone, that it is crucial for the whole church, that it should be a means of overcoming the divorce between life and faith, and should help us forward in the search for meaning in life and faith. I have tried to show the difference between theology as a living dynamic process growing out of present experience and theology as propositions handed on from the past.

8. Theology does not provide us with prescriptive answers to questions or problems. What it does provide is provisional formulations of faith that enable us to make the truth our own at a certain level in order to go forward to the next stage of

exploration. It enables a more realistic approach to living, greater openness to the reality of God in life, and mutual support and encouragement.

9. The theological task is never finished. 'The revelation is a reality that is always present. Theology is not a closed system but a living, dynamic, search for the truth, the partial success of the search only stimulating a desire to explore further and to reflect more deeply on the inexhaustible riches of Christ.'[9]

In order to try to make the argument of this chapter clear in another way, I am introducing a diagram at this point to illustrate what happens in the theological process. In addition there are some examples directly related to this chapter in the Appendix at the end of the book. You may feel it helps to look at these now, or, on the other hand, you may prefer not to interrupt the flow of the whole argument but to come back to them on a second reading.

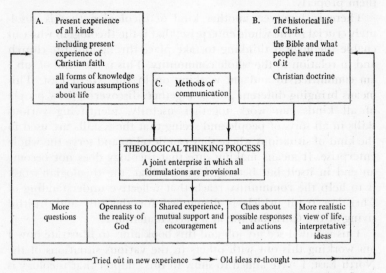

The operation of the whole in the presence and power of the Holy Spirit

Theological thinking is a perfectly normal activity that is done by anyone who consciously tries to relate faith and life. The diagram analyses what happens when we do this.

The process can start at different points but the most natural place to start is where experience of any kind disturbs us and makes us begin to ask questions. The content of theology is (A) – experience of all kinds, and – (B) an understanding of the revelation of God in Jesus Christ gained from the various Christian traditions. In order to get this varied content, theology must be done as a joint operation. This leads to difficulties in communication and, therefore, a third input – C consists of ways of communication. I have in mind the kind of contribution that is made by study of language or the skills of behavioural scientists.

The real theological work is involved in looking at life experiences in terms of revelation and looking at our understanding of revelation in the light of an honest examination of experience. An understanding of each is developed by being brought into relation with the other.

The five points on the lower line of the diagram show the outcome of theological thinking and discussion. This is emphatically not a set of answers to questions posed by life nor is it a prescriptive and final formulation of tenets of belief. The first gain from the process is mutual support and encouragement between those who take part in the process. The value and the need for this cannot be over-estimated – every Christian needs this kind of support and this should be one of the main functions of the church.

A further gain is that we go back to living with a more realistic approach to life, a greater openness to the reality of God in life and a new impetus and direction in living. We may not find answers to questions but we gain strength to live with these questions and to continue to search for meaning in life and faith.

Theology cannot be done properly within the confines of the church, but belongs to the whole sphere of operation of the Spirit of God which is the whole universe. We have been promised that it is he who will lead us not into a limited area of what is true to one individual – but 'into all truth'.

NOTES

1. Dr E. B. Pusey, 1868, quoted by I. T. Ramsey at the Church Leaders' Conference 1972.
2. Quoted by I. T. Ramsey in the same lecture.
3. J. Pieper, *Hope and History*, Burns & Oates 1969, p. 78.
4. R. P. C. Hanson in W. Nicholls, *The Pelican Guide to Modern Theology*, Penguin Books 1969, vol. 1, p. 7.
5. S. Moore, *God is a New Language*, Darton, Longman & Todd 1970, p. 169.
6. N. Pittenger, *The Christian Church as Social Process*, Epworth Press 1971, p. 90.
7. David Jenkins, Report to the Central Committee of the WCC, 1972.
8. Charles Davis in Gabriel Moran, *Theology of Revelation*, Search Press 1967, p. 11.
9. Moran, op. cit., p. 20.

IV

MISSION
is Concerned with Wholeness

There are at present deep divisions in the church about the nature of its task in the world. These divisions are usually expressed by differences about how the church should be organized, or how it should spend its money, or deploy its manpower. But behind these strategic differences there are fundamental differences of belief and different assumptions about how people may come to know God.

Some of these differences have been indicated in the discussion of revelation and theology. In this chapter I shall show how these differences extend to understandings of the nature of mission. I shall then go on to show that most understandings of mission are partial and incomplete, for mission is concerned with wholeness and with the unification of all things in Christ. We should not therefore settle for one or other of the partial views of mission that are on offer, but struggle together to enlarge our vision until we can see the grandeur, diversity, harmony and wholeness that should be our hope and goal.

It may help at this point to distinguish two main strands of thinking about all this. It is of course not possible to divide people into clearly defined groups 'for' or 'against' each point of view, but wherever Christian faith is discussed divisions arise and the following summary may help us to understand what is happening. In each case beliefs about revelation, theology and mission hang together to form distinct patterns of thinking.

One pattern of thinking assumes that people come to know God by the clear enunciation of propositions from the past, and the 'faith once delivered' is expressed in large abstract terms such as sin, judgment, repentance and redemption. The other pattern is based on the belief that God makes himself known in and through persons and events in the present in a continuing, dynamic process and that the Christian past, including the life of Jesus should be used to interpret present events.

Different understandings of theology follow. In the first case theology is seen as the study of the Bible and what people have made of it, in the second case it is seen as a continuing process of interpreting contemporary experience in the light of God's revelation in Christ. These two views lead to radically different approaches to the practise and study of theology.

There are also two views of the nature of the church; on the one hand it is seen as those who have been called out of an evil world, and their task is to obey the command to preach the gospel and to save as many souls as possible out of the world. In order to do this the church's organization is likened to that of an army, often with the implication that clergy are officers and laymen are the troops. The other view avoids making sharp distinctions between those who are 'in' or 'out' of the church and conceives that the church's job is to penetrate the world and point to the signs of God's transforming activity in the whole creation. In this more optimistic view lay people are seen as having a crucial ministry in the world with clergy as their helpers.

The differences which arise from different understandings of God and his activity culminate in different understandings of man and of Christ. The first view is concerned with man's soul and emphasizes the dangers of the body and of materialism. Man is seen as an isolated individual apart from any social context. The other view sees man as a totality in whom body and soul are inseparable and whose life only has meaning in relation to his total historical and social context. In the first view it is natural to lay stress on Christ's divinity and in the second view on his humanity.

This very rough outline of differences is summed up in the table below:

A	B
Revelation	
God is known through unchanging propositions, handed on from the past in large abstract concepts – sin, judgment, repentance, redemption, etc.	God is known by personal meeting in and through persons and events in the present

A	B

Theology
is a study of the Bible and what people have made of it

is a continuing process of interpreting contemporary experience in the light of God's revelation in Christ ...

is to be done by academic experts

is to be done by everyone

The Church
consists of those called out of an evil world

sharp distinctions between those who do or do not belong to the church are not helpful

its task is to obey the command to preach the gospel and

the church's job is to penetrate the world and point to the signs of God's activity in it

to save souls out of the world

the whole creation is to be redeemed

to do this it must build up its own organization in a disciplined way

clergy are leaders and laymen must help them

laymen have a crucial ministry in the world and clergy must help them

Man
the soul is the important part of man and he must beware of the body and materialism

man is a total person, body and spirit

man is an isolated individual

man's life only has meaning in relation to his total social and historical context

Jesus Christ
divinity is stressed

humanity is stressed.

Of course there are no pure types of either point of view, but the division is so widespread and produces such different practical approaches to the church's work that it is important to understand what is happening and why people are pulling in different directions. The two views have been called Mission 'A' corresponding to the view in the left-hand column, and Mission 'B' corresponding to the view in the right-hand column. There are some important points in Mission 'A'. It is properly trying to safeguard the fact of conflict and sin in the world. This is one way of standing for transcendence and grace. But 'A' has let everything else be dominated by the notion of sin and the result is that 'A' has withdrawn from the world, and therefore cannot save the world. By over-emphasizing conflict, sin, transcendence, grace, it has stood them on their head, and cut off the possibility of effective witness to the world.

It is my conviction that the points that are made in Mission 'B' are essential to a relevant style of mission for the whole church in our present industrial society and that a style of mission that is based on an unquestioning acceptance of 'A' cannot do the job. Yet Mission 'A' is the predominant outlook in the church today and Mission 'B' is so unfamiliar that it raises problems for most church people.

The sharp contrast between the two views is illustrated by the following conversation which took place between a parochial clergyman (whom we will call 'A' as he represents Mission 'A') and an industrial chaplain (whom we will call 'B' as he represents Mission 'B'):

A: 'I am puzzled by the way you go about your work and the things you say. I am not sure whether you are actually saying something different from me, or whether you are just saying the same things in a different way.'

B: 'I am giving such a different emphasis in my interpretation of Christian faith that it certainly strikes the average churchgoer as being quite different from what you say. Changes in the world and in our whole culture mean that we are in a new situation and must have a new message.'

A: 'But there is nothing fundamentally new today. There have always been changes, but human beings remain the same, and the main job of the church – the conversion of individuals – remains unchanged.'

B: 'You are not concerned with what happens in the world. If you really cared about people you would be concerned with the world, for human beings are part of their own society and of the whole creation. I believe this is God's world and that it is fundamentally good. The Christian task is to work with God for the removal of all that hinders the fulfilment of God's will in the world.'

A: 'My concern is to state clearly the unchanged gospel of Jesus Christ and to be true to the whole gospel. You are just picking out those bits that suit you.'

B: 'The good news must touch on a person's own experience and I make that my starting point. You are suggesting that there is nothing new to be discovered and that the job of theology is finished. I believe that theology must be the continuing task of understanding present events in the light of God's revelation in Christ. This task must be shared by all sorts of people.'

A: 'I was ordained and given authority to pass on the truth of the gospel as it is expressed in the Bible. It seems to me that you are leaning over backwards not to offend those who are not Christians and that you are straining language to minimize the difference between Christians and others.'

B: 'Of course I must use language that people understand. Traditional language that has no relation to present experience doesn't communicate anything.'

A: 'Christians must be different from other people. We have to speak out whether people accept it or not.'

B: 'God is making himself known to everyone in one way or another. He is concerned for all humanity and has shown us in Jesus' life what it can mean to be fully human.'

A: 'You leave out the divinity of Christ. God is transcendent and above the everyday things of life. We must be careful not to make man the measure of God.'

B: 'I do not want to limit God, but I do say that he is present and to be known within the daily experiences of life.'

A: 'God is known in worship and prayer. You under-estimate the place of worship. Worship, as an offering to God, is what we should be most concerned with.'

B: 'For worship to mean anything it should be that moment when man makes most explicit what is true of his whole life – that is that, in responding to God in his love, man gives the whole of his life and every part of his world a new significance and a new value because he gives it a new destiny.'

This debate is typical enough. I have set it out in some detail because it is important for us to recognize these divisions not so that we may take sides or say that either view is totally right or wrong, but so that we can press ahead to find a way out of this impasse. A way forward cannot be found by trying to prove that 'A' or 'B' has the full truth, nor by trying to find a consensus of the two views. Such an attempt to reach harmony before the final kingdom would only find a lowest common denominator and would mean death. It is more important to heighten the different insights in order to struggle together to discover something new.

Peace is the new name for mission

'Development is the new name for peace', said the Pope – and he might have added that peace is the name for mission. The theme of peace runs throughout the Bible and God's salvation is looked forward to as the establishment of peace. At first sight the word peace may not seem very helpful. I have found that many people react against words like peace, reconciliation, forgiveness, for they have been led by their experience to see these words either as weak words or representing the victory of the *status quo* and an enforced uniformity in which conflict and criticism are swept under the carpet, and the cry for justice and creativity is silenced. This refusal to recognize the realities of conflict has lead some people to stress 'liberation' as the meaning of mission.

But peace in the Bible means a great deal more than capitulation, the absence of war or the mean compromises by which we manage to avoid conflict. The fundamental meaning of the Hebrew 'shalom' or 'peace' is 'wholeness' or 'totality'. It is this comprehensive understanding of peace as the objective of mission that we need to recover. The heart of the biblical concept is the free growth of the person which can only happen in conjunction with others. This includes every kind of happiness but the kernel is community as the foundation of life. Peace has a thoroughly material basis and is seen in the Old Testament in terms of long life, prosperity, abundance, success in enterprises and victory in war. The point that we must grasp is the fact that it can only be established on the basis of truth, righteousness, justice and concern for the disadvantaged.

The understanding of peace as wholeness applies to the life of the individual as much as to the life of society. If the individual is to be at one with himself all aspects of his nature must be allowed to grow. Christian faith has often been seen as an irksome discipline which does violence to the natural self. Peace demands that we come to terms with ourselves and with all our relationships including our social and historical involvement. In other words, peace means maturity and fulfilment of the whole personality in his whole context. This can only happen where there is judgment, justice and repentance. The individual and the social working out of peace cannot be separated.

The argument about peace in the Old Testament is between a false peace founded on injustice and privilege, and a true peace which must be founded on community and justice. This inevitably involves judgment on all that is wrong and unjust. This is the point that the prophets try to drive home. The prophet Jeremiah lived at a time when the Assyrians were threatening to attack the Jews and most of the prophets were saying the soothing things people wanted to hear – 'Don't worry, it won't happen – God will look after you'. Only Jeremiah was prepared to risk his neck by pointing out the impossibility of any real peace on the basis of the Jews' current way of life:

'For from the least to the greatest of them every one is greedy for unjust gain; and from the prophet to priest, every one deals falsely. They have healed the wound of my people lightly, saying, "Peace, peace," when there is no peace' (Jer. 6.13-14).

Where there is injustice, there is need for judgment, repentance and forgiveness and for this reason peace is seen as a gift from God, and as the salvation for which the Jews hoped. This hope is expressed by the prophet Isaiah, and Christians see its fulfilment in the person of Jesus Christ:

'For unto us a child is born, to us a son is given; and the government will be upon his shoulder, and his name will be called "Wonderful Counsellor, Mighty God, Everlasting Father, Prince of Peace".

'Of the increase of his government and of peace there will be no end, upon the throne of David, and over his kingdom, to establish it, and to uphold it with justice and with righteousness from this time forth and for evermore. The zeal of the Lord of hosts will do this' (Isa. 9.6-7).

This understanding of mission as peace, and of the true nature of peace must be an integral part of our whole understanding of the Christian task in the world. Concern for the third world, for inequalities and injustices in our society, for industrial relations and for immigrants is a vital part of the church's mission. There can be no mission unless it includes these things. At this point it is worth referring back to the discussion between 'A' and 'B' in the earlier part of this chapter. The fact that 'A', a parochial clergyman, was puzzled by the activities of 'B', an industrial chaplain, suggests that 'A' had not understood the full meaning of mission. This common lack of understanding is often expressed by the following set of comments being made to those working in industrial mission or social responsibility:

'What are you doing that an industrial welfare officer or social worker could not do?' or 'Why don't you go into politics?'

A further lack of understanding of the wholeness of salvation is expressed, when it is suggested that a concern with justice, and peace is pre-evangelistic and that it is simply a preparation for the preaching of the gospel. This suggestion not only fails to understand the gospel as a gospel of wholeness but also fails to see the integral nature of the Old and New Testaments. It suggests that Jesus did away with the old covenant rather than fulfilling it. Christ is our peace (Eph. 2.14). The Old Testament theme of peace is given a new clarity in the New Testament, and the Epistle to the Ephesians sums up what it means to say that peace is the name for mission.

Christ was raised to life by the Spirit of God and filled with his life-giving power. 'This reality overflows the limitations of his historic manhood, and now gives life to the world. Christ becomes many while remaining one, and the many become one in Him, while remaining themselves.'[1] It is the risen life of Christ that all Christians share; this life continues to flow outwards embracing more and more individual persons and cultures, it carries the ability to transcend one's own limitations and to communicate with – even to exist for – others.

'Christ's work, in other words, and the work of the Church which prolongs it, is a work of unification, of making the nations into a single People of God. It is a work which breaks down barriers between individuals and groups, all the discriminatory barriers which divide races religions, classes, nationalities and even sexes.'[2] The epistle takes the hostility between Jews and Gentiles as an example of this unification and says:

'He is our peace, who has made us both one, and has broken down the dividing wall of hostility, by abolishing in His flesh the law of commandments and ordinances, that He might create in Himself one new man in place of the two so making peace, and might reconcile us both to God in one body through the cross, thereby bringing the hostility to an end' (Eph. 2.14-16).

' "Making the many one" is a contradiction in terms for everyone except the Christian who has really understood Christ. Unification does not mean forcing uniformity, reducing everything to a single blueprint or common denominator. Unification is not "a conquest of the nations" for Christ, a spiritual form of imperialism. It means spreading the mentality of co-operation, mutual understanding, optimism, justice and the desire for peace. It means the union of everyone in the desire for the good of each other, in ultimate respect for each other. In short, it means love, and the Spirit with which the risen Christ was anointed is the Spirit of Love.'[3] It is only selfless love that respects the differences of individuals, groups and nations; and love only realizes its full nature where there are real differences. This quality of love is a gift that comes to us as we find oneness with Christ. It is not an intellectual thing but must be lived by spending oneself for others.

But Christian life is a receiving as well as a giving, a discovering as well as a telling. We do not simply take Christ with us to those who do not know him, but we seek to discern the new expressions of Christ in different cultures and peoples. The bigot who thinks he knows it all is as undesirable as the lady bountiful who thinks she has it all, and we must be aware of our own need of others as well as of their need of us. In St Paul's meditation on the meaning of mission he comes to the conclusion that there is no possibility of the fullness of salvation being experienced by one nation let alone one individual by himself (Rom. 9-11).

The one new man that is being formed is the fullness of Christ himself. The goal is that we shall 'all attain to the unity of the faith and of the knowledge of the Son of God, to mature manhood, to the measure of the stature of the fullness of Christ' (Eph. 4.13).

In and through his death Christ established with his church an understanding of mutual and total self-giving. Through this understanding, which is of course only grasped in living experience, the whole of humanity and all creation is to be drawn into a unity created by relationships of mutual and total self-giving. The church's task and mission is to be the present sign and the instrument of the unity of all mankind.

At this stage in our discussion of the church's task we may point to the kind of priorities this view of mission suggests.

The Holy Spirit is active and present throughout the whole creation and it is he who opens up the possibilities of mission:

'The chief actor in the historic mission of the Christian church is the Holy Spirit. He is the director of the whole enterprise. The mission consists of the things that he is doing in the world. In a special way it consists of the light that he is focussing upon Jesus Christ.'[4] This means an openness to the unexpected, a provisional quality in all our plans combined with a readiness that comes from the fact that we have done our homework and are alert to the possibilities of the future, rather than being tied to the past.

Too often the Holy Spirit has been invoked as an excuse for not giving our attention to the factors of our present situation, and not following through the obvious implications that should derive from an honest and intelligent understanding of Christian faith. From our discussion, two important dimensions of mission stand out:

'The first dimension is the horizontal one – expansion. This does not mean necessarily numerical expansion, but it does mean that the Church must be continually entering areas where Christ is not explicitly acknowledged, and re-entering areas where, due to radical changes, the knowledge of Christ has been forgotten. We are not talking here of a strictly spatio-temporal expansion, therefore, but of a continual journey through the multiple changing circumstances of man. It is a continual identification with, and adaptation to, successive personal, social and cultural experiences. Such experiences have extension, of course, in space and time, but the emphasis is on the variety, the multiplicity of experiences.'[5]

In practical terms, for instance, this would mean that the church must take steps to relate to specific aspects of man's life such as – work, leisure, home, politics, and, in view of the international nature of industrial society, with his international relations.

If the church is to be a present sign of the unity of mankind it must take this kind of step in order to redress its present imbalances. When I was in Hong Kong, for example, we analysed the membership of four congregations in an industrial area and found that the majority were students or retired people. I shall say more later about the particular imbalances of the church in the North East.

The second dimension is one of penetration. To a limited extent there are Christians – lay people or clergy in the main areas of life, work, leisure, home, politics, etc.; but it isn't enough just to be there, we must go further and ask what role they are fulfilling as Christians in these areas of life. The knowledge of Christ should enable us to penetrate more deeply into the meaning of what is happening, to probe and to understand our environment from every angle, to question and assess values and goals in the light of the humanization of God's world and the creation of peace. This kind of penetration into the different levels and facets of human life requires the development and use of people's talents and all that nature offers. The command to 'fill the earth and subdue it' (Gen. 1.28) means that both nature and technology must be re-stored in Christ. The need for this kind of penetration follows from the deep understanding of peace which we have tried to draw out. It involves a right attitude to the material world, a search for justice, an awakening of the consciences of the rich, and a questioning of the goals and assumptions of society.

This discussion may be summed up by saying that peace or wholeness is the goal of mission, wholeness for the individual, wholeness for society, wholeness for the creation, wholeness that is only possible in Christ who is our peace. I believe this affirmation could be a starting point for further discussion between the different views of mission that are at present impairing the church's wholeness and effectiveness. I do not however think that we can leave the matter there, for perhaps one of the most divisive issues concerns the nature of the Christian responsibility in society and it is to that issue that we must now turn.

NOTES

1. Aylward Shorter, *Theology of Mission*, Mercier Press 1972, p. 34.
2. Shorter, op. cit., p. 35.
3. Ibid.
4. J. V. Taylor, *The Go-Between God*, SCM Press 1972, p. 3.
5. Shorter, op. cit., p. 36.

V

PROPHECY
a Ministry to Society

The church has a prophetic ministry to society as such, to institutions as well as to individuals. In fact individuals cannot discover meaning in life except as members of society. One of the main differences between the two views of mission described in the last chapter is that 'A' emphasizes a ministry to individuals in isolation, while 'B' sees the need for a ministry to society as such. In this chapter I want to transcend these divisions by presenting a clearer picture of what is meant by a ministry to society.

Industrialization and the social changes it causes raise fundamental problems for the church's traditional understanding of ministry. Many people are confused because they have not grasped the fact that the old model of ministry is inappropriate today. For the Church of England, at least, the traditional model is that of a clergyman living in a clearly defined community in which he has pastoral responsibility for each individual in all aspects of his life. In the face of the impersonal nature of industrial society the church clings to this model as a way of affirming the unique character of each individual. But this important point must be made in some other way for the old model cannot be applied in the kind of urban situation that industrialization produces. The sheer size of the populations of Tyneside (well over 1,000,000), Teesside (400,000) and Sunderland (200,000) for example make the old kind of pastoral relationship impossible. Nor is it just a matter of numbers, for in this kind of society individuals are not simply related to a local community, but to a community of work, education, leisure, politics and civic affairs, each of which has its own institutional framework which extends over a much larger area than the immediate residential community.

These changes in society raise identity problems for the individual who must discover the meaning of his relationships with these institutions if he is to discover the meaning of his own life.

The size and power of these groupings makes the individual feel powerless and de-personalized. This is why the development of new forms of participation are so important, and why the church must recognize that the old paternalistic relationship in its own life will not do in today's world.

It is important to point out that the situation has not only changed for the towns but also for the country. However remote the villages and farms may seem, it must be clear that the changes that are taking place in the countryside cannot be understood apart from industrialization. Industrial society is a totality and, if it is negative about the uniqueness of the individual, it is positive about the solidarity of all mankind. These changes are forcing us to re-think the nature of the church's ministry to society.

Two views of the church's ministry to society

The different views of mission 'A' and 'B' inevitably lead to different understandings of the church's ministry to society. Stated in their extreme forms, the difference amounts to a fundamental difference in understanding Christian faith itself.

'A' is world denying. In this view God saves people out of the world and the creation itself has no ultimate significance. 'A' is therefore only concerned with movements of history or changes in society in as far as they directly affect the church's task.

'A' sees man as a sojourner in this world. His responsibility is not to change the world, but to play out his own role within it, and according to how he does this his life in a world beyond will be determined. In this view there can be no ministry to society as such, for the world is simply a backdrop to man's activities and to his progress to a purely spiritual salvation.

'B' is world affirming – believing that God is active in the world and that his purposes include the whole creation. 'B' is therefore concerned with the world, with history, with human society and with all that can help the full development of humanity. He believes that Christians are called to co-operate with God in his work of transforming the whole creation. A serious concern with a ministry to society must follow. The church's task is then seen as declaring Christ's Lordship over all things, the reconciliation of men with each other as well as with God, and as changing society itself so that, instead of hindering, it assists this end.

The crucial difference is that 'A' stresses the isolated individual and his individual response to God, while 'B' always sees man in his whole social and historical context, believes that response must be in terms of that specific context, and that the solidarity of humanity requires a community response.

I have already pointed out that the church's present thinking is deeply influenced by the individualism of 'A', and for this reason 'B's emphasis on the need for a ministry to society seems strange and unfamiliar. We have only to open our Bibles, however, to see that the prophetic ministry is essential to a full understanding of the meaning of Christian faith.

A prophetic ministry

The Old Testament prophets were world-affirming. What was happening in the world mattered, because it is God's world and he is concerned with everyone and with all events. What the prophets said refers to the actual events of their own time. Their message is not addressed to individuals but to nations and groups, from whom response is demanded in terms of their own concrete and immediate situation.

The prophet Jeremiah lived near Jerusalem at a time when Assyria was a growing threat to the small Jewish state. Jeremiah was not a professional prophet and had no desire to be one, but he came to believe that he must speak in God's name about the meaning of what was happening. He saw the threat from Assyria as a warning to the people of Jerusalem, which should lead them to the kind of repentance and change that would create a juster society:

'Warn the nations that he is coming; announce to Jerusalem, Besiegers come from a distant land. . . .

'Your ways and your doings have brought this upon you' (Jer. 4.16, 18).

'For from the least to the greatest of them, everyone is greedy for unjust gain; and from prophet to priest, everyone deals falsely' (Jer. 4.13).

'Now therefore say to the men of Judah and the inhabitants of Jerusalem: Thus says the Lord, Behold I am shaping evil against you and devising a plan against you. Return every one from his evil way, and amend your ways and your doings' (Jer. 18.11).

What Jeremiah says is stimulated by actual events, but his reaction goes beyond superficial interpretations, for he sees these events in the light of a deep commitment to God's purpose for human life.

Nor is he a detached observer but is very much a member of his own community and nation. It is this commitment to God and to the world that heightens both his insight and his agony.

It is important to point out that the prophets do not call people to a religious revival but to radical changes in their way of life so that their lives would in themselves be witness to God's nature of truth, love and justice. Without this kind of integrity of life, religious observance is utter blasphemy. Our own loss of any sense of belonging leads us to think of the prophets as lonely figures, but in fact they saw themselves as members of their own nation; what they said was addressed to their nation and to particular groups in it, and called them to fulfil their own particular role in human history.

The prophets assumed that the people they spoke to had some idea of what they were talking about. They took hold of popular ideas, and re-shaped them often turning them upside down. For instance the Jews looked forward to 'a good time coming' which they thought of as 'the Day of the Lord', but the prophets pointed out that if there was to be 'a Day of the Lord' it must mean that injustice and oppression would finally be brought out into the open and dealt with – and that might be very uncomfortable for them. The prophets would have been incomprehensible and irrelevant if they had not tackled the attitudes that had been built into the fabric of their own society. Any ministry to society must speak to the particular traditions that are currently embodied in that society and its various groupings and must tackle the actual situations of that particular time. The work of prophecy is then to open up the possibilities of the future and show what action must be taken in the present. Hope for the future is always a part of the prophet's message, but it is a hope that can only be realized through fundamental change – repentance. The hope that is held out is the establishment of God's rule of peace – 'shalom' – that will bring the whole creation into unity. For the Jews this hope was conceived first of all as the establishment of a rule of peace in their own land. Many disappointments made it clear that this hope could not finally be identified with any particular political state of affairs. Every actual rule proved inadequate and to identify the final kingdom with what actually obtained would have been to close the door to further development and growth. Until the end of time there must be a tension between what is and what could be, but this should not mean that the hope of the Kingdom of God is detached from concrete historical action.

Christians believe that Jesus created the conditions under which prophetic hopes could be fulfilled. It is not a matter of contrasting a personal ministry of Jesus with the social message of the prophets, for Jesus' preaching fufilled the prophetic tradition – 'Repent for the Kingdom of Heaven is at hand' (Mark 1.14). His challenge, like that of the prophets, was to the leaders of the Jews telling them to accept the radical implications of their own tradition and to enable the nation to respond to its true vocation. The polarization between individual and society, between world-affirming and world-denying, between this world and some future world must be transcended by seeing that salvation operates on several different levels at once, and that these levels are inter-related. In other words peace – 'shalom' – salvation must be seen as an integral matter:

'The initial and fundamental issue, however, is the unity of the divine vocation and therefore of the destiny of man, of all men. The historical point of view allows us to break out of the narrow, individualistic viewpoint and see with more Biblical eyes that men are called to meet the Lord insofar as they constitute a community, a people. It is a question not so much of a vocation to salvation as a convocation.'[1]

A prophetic ministry to society should not be seen as one aspect of ministry to be contrasted with a ministry to individuals, but as the way in which all ministry is to be understood and the meaning of life and faith is summed up. Though the line of prophecy has often been no more than a thread, it has continued both inside and outside the church up to our own day.

It may be salutary to recall that, although the Old Testament prophets were rejected in their own day, their message provided the living seeds of the future.

A prophetic ministry today

Today world events are forcing us to ask urgent questions about the meaning of life and to see these questions in world terms. Things which have seemed stable are undergoing radical change. If ever there was a time for prophecy it is now – but the church does not find this type of ministry natural to its present stance and style.

On a number of occasions I have sat down with church groups and asked them to list the main questions that they think are important to the people in their locality. The lists they have produced have been markedly different from lists that have been contributed by non-church groups. A typical church list includes:

Pornography, abortion, homosexuality, religious education,

vandalism, youth, and the elderly.

A typical secular list on the other hand includes:

The economy, scientific and technical change, race relations, employment and unemployment, politics and participation in local planning, industrial relations, new styles of management and authority.

Here we have another dichotomy. We have already seen that there are two views of revelation, two styles of theology and two different understandings of mission. Now we have two different perceptions of what the main questions of a community are. Each list emerges from a different perspective on life. Behind the thinking of those who produced the church list is the Mission 'A' theological position. This sees the aim of the church as that of saving individuals out of the world. Its main concern is with the purity of personal morality and the education of individuals in the tenets of Christian faith and personal behaviour. It is concerned to see that people get the 'right' kind of information and that help is given to the needy, but it does not see the church's business as that of co-operating with God in the transformation of the world. It therefore fails to grasp the essence of Christian faith with its belief in God's action within the creation for the redemption of all things.

It is this fundamental misunderstanding of the nature of Christian faith that must be tackled. Until this is done any appeal to Christians to take their social responsibilities seriously will fall on deaf ears and the church will not be released to fulfil its proper role in the world.

As it is church members have been conditioned to assume that their faith is relevant to some areas of life and not to others. They include in their concerns – personal morality, some obvious social needs and face to face relationships, but exclude areas of conflict especially politics and aspects of life not directly concerned with face to face relationships – such as economics, or where questions are too technical and difficult for anyone to be able to pronounce a clear right or wrong.

Those who drew up the secular list recognized facts that should be obvious to anyone who looks honestly at our present situation – that is that technology and industry shape our society and not Victorian moralism. If technology is not to destroy us we must control it so that it contributes to human fulfilment. We must master technology instead of being its slaves. This is the nettle that must be grasped, and if Christians do not concern themselves with this, everything else they do will simply be 'fiddling while Rome burns'. If, however, we are prepared to tackle these main questions of our society it does mean that we should not care about the elderly, or about pornography or abortion. What it does mean is that we must see these things in a bigger context.

The difference in the two lists of concerns points to the need for a revolution in the church's whole attitude to society, and by 'revolution' – I mean 'revolution'. This does not mean that Christians should be at every demonstration, but that we have to change ourselves as people. In order to spell out what this means I must remind you of the differences among Christians that I have already described:

Revelation can be seen either as giving information or as effecting transformation. In the latter view, which is the view I follow, God makes himself known to people with the result, not that they have some extra information, but that they are in some way changed persons. It is of the essence of God's nature to transform all that he touches, and he calls men to co-operate with him in the transformation of the whole world. This must include our technological society and all its activities.

Conflict and disturbance cannot be avoided if there is to be change. In fact, that is the main problem of change – it upsets things. People who work in industry know this only too well, for they have to cope with the tensions and sufferings that are involved in closing down a plant or changing styles of management. Some who live with this kind of tension understand their experience as a kind of crucifixion, and it is strange that Christians often fail to see that commitment to Christ must involve challenges to the *status quo* that make conflict inevitable.

Theology does not provide ready-made answers. The questions of society are too complex for rule-of-thumb judgments, and we have to learn to live with tensions and confusions in which there are only many shades of grey, but this does not mean that we should do nothing. What it does mean is that we must take theology seriously as something that we have to work at together in order to discover what God is saying to us in a particular situation and what steps towards the transformation of all things can be taken here and now. Naturally we shall not all agree, and the more we care the more we may disagree, but this is the only way to progress, and action does not have to wait for universal agreement.

Mission means involvement and it is as we become involved that God will make himself known to us. It is in this meeting

with God that revolution happens – for revolution is a turning
and a repentance from self-concern and towards social-concern.
Repentance means a change of centre – a complete re-orientation
so that we cease to be engrossed in our own concerns and are
able to look outward and to become aware of the needs of others.
When this revolution happens the church's list of priorities will
change.

Practical priorities of a ministry to society

Without much detail, I want to point to a few practical
priorities that follow from this understanding of a ministry to
society:

1. First – a prophetic ministry must start from a genuine concern
with the world for itself, and only then go on to ask what place the
church might have. We noticed, when we compared the two lists
of concerns, that the first list started from a position in which the
church was at the centre, so that aspects of the world's life came
into focus only insofar as they seemed important for the church
and its concerns. The second list was completely different because
it started with the world and its affairs as the central point. As
long as the church starts with itself as the centre, it will not meet
the needs of the world but only respond to its own need to express
itself in some way.

2. Secondly, a ministry to society must see lay people as the
chief agents of mission. The fact that a lay person is sharing in
the life of society at a particular point by reason of his or her
occupation and daily relationships is a potential asset. But it is
not enough simply to point to the fact that lay people are present
in the various aspects of society, they must also be aware of the
significance of their position for God's purpose of the unification
of all things in Christ. For example, Gordon is training manager
in a large firm. Owing to a reduction in the number of employees
he had fewer trainees to deal with. This made it possible to create
a new kind of training scheme for unemployed youths. The idea
was developed in co-operation with the youth employment officer,
the industrial chaplain and the company. A number of unemployed youths were taken on for six months' training. Gordon
considered that this was too short a time but it was the maximum
that the government would finance.

The youths were given an introduction to engineering work
and Gordon found most of them jobs to go to. He felt the course
needed to be developed and paid a number of visits to the House
of Commons and to other government officials and has gained

agreement and finance for some of the improvements he wants, including an extension of the course to one year.

Planning and carrying out the course has led to a development in Gordon's own thinking about the kind of things that young people need to learn if they are to take part in the world of work. These include much more than technical skills – some understanding of economics, a new understanding of the place of work in life, of human relationships and so on. These issues raise fundamental questions about the meaning of human life and how it can be lived satisfactorily. Gordon has been able to make these changes because his job in industry puts him in a position to take this kind of initiative. If the world is to be transformed it can only be done from within.

This insistence on the importance of the lay person in his secular role should not suggest that the clergy are less important than before. Gordon gained a vision of the possibilities of his situation and encouragement to do what he did from the industrial chaplain working in his firm and none of us can work entirely on our own. What this does mean, however, is that the church has a lot of work to do if it is to release the full potential of its members. In the first place it means a reversal of the common understanding of the clergy/lay relationship, so that it is recognized that the job of the clergy is to help lay people perform their mission, in the world, rather than lay people helping clergy to perform their job in the church. This change of relationship is more shattering than you might think. I am tempted to compare it in potential explosiveness to the relationship of nationals and colonists on the eve of liberation.

3. A further point that must be emphasized is that Christians must be concerned with the structures of society as such. It is a complete fallacy to think that if enough individuals are converted it will follow as a natural consequence that society will also be transformed. Unfortunately, this fallacy is built into the church's thinking.

At a time when people were suffering from the worst conditions of the Industrial Revolution, Wilberforce, the great evangelical parliamentarian, proposed that all that was needed was for each person to discharge diligently 'the duties of his own station ... and all would be active and harmonious in the goodly frame of human society'. This kind of appeal to people to live by the secondary virtues of duty and obedience without taking into account the prophetic call to tackle the fundamental causes of injustice is simply a way of giving support to the *status quo*. Any ministry to society must be consciously concerned with changes in institutions themselves.

Syd is secretary of a hospital board. He is concerned with healing and his particular way of showing this is that of an administrator. He is anxious that each individual in the community should have his needs met and he realizes that this can only be done if there are proper channels of communication between the patients and their relatives and the whole administration. He is therefore deeply concerned in the re-organization of the health service and is working to make sure that representation on the new committees effectively ensures that the patient's own needs can be heard. He realizes that the approach that sees the individual in isolation will not in the end meet their needs but that there must be a concern with changing institutions as well as changing individuals and that these changes are inextricably tied together. A sense of powerlessness in relation to the large institutions of society is common to most people. Syd is in a comparatively strong position to influence change, but a person at the bottom of the scale can only influence change if he is prepared to work with others in some kind of organization or action group.

4. Any suggestion, however, that a concern with structures is opposed to a ministry to individuals is quite wrong. It is only when structures are taken seriously that there can be a proper ministry to the individuals in them.

For example, Maureen, who is a local councillor, when speaking to a group of students, said:

'I am a Christian and it is my Christian faith that has led me to become involved in politics, but my local church cannot help me to withstand the temptation to misuse the very considerable power I have; it cannot help me to consider the needs of all the people in my area. For that I need someone who has a closer understanding of the exact nature of these questions.'

As it happens, Maureen is in touch with a clergyman, who has been appointed to do social responsibility work in the area and is spending much of his time with local councillors and officials. It is because he has an overall view of what is happening in local politics, that he is able to show a new kind of pastoral concern which takes into account the pressures of her public life as a councillor as well as her private role as a wife and mother.

Maureen's comments point to the need for things to be done at various levels of the church's life, but none of these will happen unless there is a recognition of the importance of politics, industry, and economics for the church's whole mission. The real issues are not obvious from outside, and the church must appoint more people to give their whole time to work in these particular fields and to help the rest of the church understand the issues that are involved. If clergy are to help lay people like Gordon, Syd and Maureen, they can't do it from a distance – this surely is one of the lessons of the incarnation.

An example of prophecy today

At the time of writing there is a world energy crisis, which has been brought to a head by changes in policy by the oil producing countries, and in Britain by a coal mining dispute. The fact that people are being personally inconvenienced makes them more ready to ask what it all means and we must ask 'What does a prophetic ministry mean in this situation?'

First of all it means facing the truth, and not crying 'Peace, peace,' where there is no peace. Those who are knowledgeable about world energy supplies and uses did not need these events to alert them to the pending energy crisis. They had been trying for some time to get people to understand the limitations of all natural resources and the folly of continuing growth policies. Yet parliamentarians and others are already trying to prove that things are not as bad as they seem, and that it is only a matter of getting through a few difficult years before Britain becomes independent as regards energy supplies. This is an attempt to avoid facing the real questions and it is the prophetic task to help people to think more deeply and radically about the meaning of what is happening and what ought to be done before it is too late.

The second need is to help people to see things whole. A number of different questions are inter-related but each group has its own particular solution or concern. It is not enough to think simply in terms of conservation, nuclear power, unilateral agreements or whatever. We must try to see the inter-relationship of all these problems and possibilities in terms of world community, the demands of justice and the stewardship and sharing of the world's resources.

It is natural for us to be most concerned with things that are happening on our own doorstep, which we feel we might be able to influence in some way. Those of us who live in the North East feel directly involved in what is happening in the coal industry and less concerned with the Middle East. But in fact people should now be able to see that things that are happening abroad are having a direct influence on local issues. World wide and local concerns are coming closer together. For instance the miners of Britain are at present in a position of power largely because of events in the oil producing countries. At this moment both the NUM and the Arabs face the same kind of question about how to use their power, and the decisions that are made will directly affect both parties.

This inter-relation of events on the two levels means that if a prophetic ministry is to be effective local ministries need to be related to activities at the national and international levels.

For instance, industrial missions are at work on the local level in a number of places in Britain and something over one hundred full-time chaplains are employed. But there is no adequate machinery for the issues that are raised locally to be taken up at national and international level. I am not forgetting the British Council of Churches Industrial Advisory Group, the C of E Industrial Committee or the WCC Urban/Industrial Mission Desk, but these organizations cannot do much until the church as a whole takes industry and politics seriously and this it is far from doing at present.

At the local level in the North East region I am personally involved with issues raised by the massive effects of technological change on employment patterns and expectations, the region's relationship with national government, local government changes and efforts to develop new forms of participation, the need for radical changes in educational policy and so on. This kind of involvement is a constant check on easy generalizations, but this little bit of experience and insight needs to be taken up into a fundamental critique of the basis and presuppositions of indust- rial society and related to the particular questions that appear at other levels both nationally and internationally.

This need means that we must be more perceptive in answering the question: 'Who is it that must exercise prophetic ministry?' The answer is obviously 'the whole church'. It is true that church leaders have a responsibility to speak for the church on certain occasions, but if this is to go beyond platitudinous generalities it must be backed up by prophetic understanding at other levels of the church's life and it really should not be only bishops and clergy who speak, but lay people also.

Prophecy cannot simply be sparked off by a TV programme or newspaper headlines, but must arise from the continuous concern at all levels with the meaning of daily events. A prophetic ministry must keep issues before people's minds after the first shock has worn off and when these issues are anything but dramatic. If we really care, we shall realize that change is not easy for any of us to accept because in the end it means becoming a different kind of person. There is an important job for the church to provide the kind of pastoral care that can enable people to receive the prophetic message of salvation. This means creating sustaining communities that do more than is being done in the present kind of congregational life. Maureen pointed to this need, and although her need was in fact met by the social responsibility officer, it should have been possible for her to find some of the understanding and support she needed within her local congregation. The local congregation must itself become prophetic in its concern for the issues of the world.

We must endeavour to transcend the polarities that at present exist between the two positions 'A' and 'B'. In doing this we shall reject the view that the church is an ark of salvation into which to escape from the world's conflicts, but we shall also reject any suggestion that the church or Christians should lose any distinguishable identity. We shall affirm the fact that to be a Christian is to co-operate with God's activity in the world, and that this means that the heart of Christian faith is a concern for the world and for the unity of all things in Christ.

So far I have been setting out these basic beliefs. I must now go back to the actual community we started out with – where Bob, John, Fergus and Jonathan belong – and I must describe that community in greater depth, for that is the context of the North East of England in which I am struggling with others to discover the full meaning of these beliefs. But first this chapter ends with a modern parable.[2]

There was once a factory which employed thousands of people. Its production line was a miracle of modern engineering, turning out thousands of machines every day. The factory had a high accident rate. The complicated machinery of the production line took little account of human error, forgetfulness, or ignorance. Day after day, men came out of the factory with squashed fingers, cuts, bruises. Sometimes a man could lose an arm or a leg. Occasionally someone was electrocuted or crushed to death.

Enlightened people began to see that something needed to be done. First on the scene were the churches. An enterprising minister organized a small first aid tent outside the factory gate. Soon, with the backing of the Council of Churches, it grew into a properly built clinic, able to give first aid to quite serious cases, and to treat minor injuries. The town council became interested, together with local bodies like the Chamber of Trade and the Rotary Club. The clinic grew into a small hospital, with modern equipment, an operating theatre, and a full time staff of doctors and nurses. Several lives were saved. Finally, the factory management, seeing the good that was being done, and wishing to prove itself enlightened, gave the hospital its official backing, with unrestricted access to the factory, a small annual grant, and an ambulance to speed serious cases from workshop to hospital ward.

But year by year, as production increased, the accident rate continued to rise. More and more men were hurt or maimed. And in spite of everything the hospital could do, more and more people died from the injuries they received. Only then did some people begin to ask if it was enough to treat people's injuries, while leaving untouched the machinery that caused them.

NOTES

1. Gustavo Gutierrez, *A Theology of Liberation*, Orbis Books 1973 and SCM Press 1974, p. 71.
2. Brian Wren, 'The Facts on World Poverty', a leaflet produced by Christian Aid.

THE CONTEXT

VI

ONE DIVIDED WORLD
The North East

I have been setting out some of the main issues that are involved in the struggle for meaning in life and faith – wherever that struggle takes place. Now I must describe the context in which I am sharing in this struggle – and this leads me back to where I began this book – the community to which Bob, John, Fergus and Jonathan belong – that is the North East, which includes Northumberland, Durham and parts of Yorkshire. I cannot give a detailed analysis of that community, but what I want to do is to show that beliefs and understandings develop within particular societies and that as conditions change so these beliefs also develop and change. In order to do that I shall simply highlight some of the things that strike me as being important in the particular circumstances of the North East.

The North East is completely unknown to many people and it has been said that for the Southerner 'The North begins at Potters Bar'. This division between North and South goes back a long way. It was the South of England that was invaded from Europe and developed, while for centuries the North was no more than a sparsely populated land of mountains and fortresses. 'Only one hundred and fifty years ago did this area spring to life. Towns doubled their population every twenty-five years. Lack of planning then forces wholesale renewal now. Boom towns were located on coal fields by swift flowing streams, both factors irrelevant in the late twentieth century. Whole industries dominating these areas are in rapid decline – mining, shipbuilding, railways and steel.... The extraordinary concentration of both economic and political power in one city (London) severely damages all the regions furthest from the capital. Unemployment here is always at least twice the national average.... The astonishing thing is that such massive neglect of whole regions could have gone on for such a long time. Even more amazing is the way those who suffered most complained so little.'[1] 'The earliest regional organizations in the country were generated in the North East, on the initiative of Dan Smith and other local leaders, in their determination to fight back during the grim winter of 1961-62 when the regional unemployment figures mounted to 43,400, the highest since the war.... The first to be set up was the North East Development Council.'[2]

This action made explicit what for many reasons had always been true of Northumberland, Durham and that part of Yorkshire that is included in Teesside, that whether they like it or not – their fortunes are linked to each other. The NEDC was only the first of a number of other regional organizations. The government's division of the country into eight economic regions did not come until 1964 – and although they included Cumberland and Westmorland in a larger Northern region, it is in the smaller North East region that I was appointed to work.

Two fundamental features of the region are highlighted by the actual setting up of the NEDC. First, it makes clear that industry is a main determining factor in society, for it was unemployment and the effects of technological change that made the different parts of the region come together.

Secondly, it brings out the natural unity of the North East by reason of its geographical features with the Scottish border as a limit to the north and the Pennine hills to the west. But at the same time it brings into the open the divisions and rivalries especially between the communities centred on the three rivers, Tyne, Wear and Tees. This rivalry was not diminished by the establishment of Newcastle as a regional capital.

It is these two features – industry and its technological changes and the unity and rivalries of the area that we must examine in more detail if we are to understand the struggle for meaning in this particular region.

Industry in the North East is based on two main factors. The first factor is the coal deposits in the counties of Northumberland and Durham. On Tyneside the coal industry had been a 'going concern' for centuries. Here the river provided the necessary means of transport, but in Durham the real development of the coalfield was necessarily linked to the development of the railways. Even so it was these two counties that took the lead in coal mining and it was for this reason that many of the inventions of the Industrial Revolution – railways, safety in mines, much marine engineering – were pioneered in the North East.

Secondly, the long line of sea coast and the rivers flowing to it facilitate transport, communications and the development of all kinds of shipping and sea-going industries and ventures.

It was this potential that sprang to life with the Industrial Revolution. 'Coal begat locomotive and locomotive begat more coal and more coal begat more industries. Commercial enterprise eagerly seized its opportunities and experiment and invention hastened to its assistance. In 1812 there were twenty shipyards at Sunderland, in 1833 there were thirty-four; in 1827 Mr Walker of Stockton invented the friction match; in 1831 the first coals were shipped at Seaham "amidst the firing of cannon and the cheering of about five thousand people"; ... in 1840 the iron works at Consett were opened, and in 1853 at Tudhoe; in 1850 mechanical coal cutters were first used and in the same year was formed the "River Tyne Improvement Commission".... In the whole of the eighteenth century there were approximately sixty boring and sinking operations for coal; in the first half, only, of the nineteenth, about two hundred and sixty.'[3]

An influx of workers came from Scotland and Yorkshire to do many of the skilled and managerial tasks and from Ireland to do the labouring and unskilled work involved in sinking mines, building docks and laying down railways. The population of the region more than doubled in the fifty years between 1831 and 1881. This increase was located in the new mining settlements and in urban concentrations on the Tyne, Wear and Tees.

Coal, railways, docks, steel, shipbuilding, engineering and construction, these industries created the industrial revolution in the North East.

All change

But all this is changing and today the new struggles with the old, the present with the past in order to create the future.

So radical is the change from old to new that it seems we may face the same kind of polarities that have been described in the earlier part of this book. Our conclusion is the same – that we must struggle with *all* the possibilities in order to transcend the polarities and create something new. To help us to do this I will present these polarities as sharply as possible.

Boom and slump has been a continuing contrast in the North East. During lean times there is a kind of grim patience that says, 'Hold on until this phase has passed and things will be better again.' But in fact things do not return to what they were as the history of Jarrow illustrates:

'When Sir Charles founded the business (Palmer's shipyard) in 1851 ... the only house standing between the hall and St Paul's Church was a farm ... and Jarrow was a small colliery village. In 1900 ... the village had become an industrial town with 40,000 inhabitants.... In 1934 the Jarrow yard was closed down as redundant. So the town became a derelict area.'[4]

Of course this is not the whole story and Jarrow today has a new lease of life, but the point has to be made that industry never stays still, its changes are not reversible, and the idea that 'one day things will return to normal' is not a philosophy that we can live by.

The second contrast and the fundamental cause of most of the other changes is between the old traditional, heavy industries that are now in decline, and the new science-based lighter industries coming into the region. This is Industrial Revolution Stage II and it augers a very different kind of future for the North East.

A great deal is said about the numbers of new jobs provided as new firms come into the region. This is important, but it tends to take attention away from other equally important questions. The changes that are taking place are not just a matter of how many jobs there are, but also of what kind of jobs and where they are. The factor that, in my opinion, could make most change in the character of the region is the change in management and control that is bound up with the fact that many of the new firms are subsidiaries often of multi-national companies. This fact needs a lot more study than it has so far received, for it provides one of the major contrasts between the old and the new and can deeply influence the quality of relationships in the area.

The development of the chemical industry in the North East is an example of what I mean. This industry was first established as far as this region is concerned on the Tyne and the Wear, but in the early part of this century it moved to the Tees. In 1923 ICI opened its works at Billingham on Teesside and it now employs some 30,000 in its two Teesside works. This, however, is only part of the chemical industry on Teesside for on Seal Sands alone, where 1,750 acres of land are being reclaimed to provide room for industrial development near the mouth of the Tees, there are at least three American chemical plants – Monsanto Textiles Ltd, Lennig Chemical Co. and W. R. Grace. This is in addition to plants like the ICI-Phillips Refinery, British Titan Products Ltd and so on. The same trend is to be seen in the fact that many of the pharmaceutical chemical industries now established on the Tyne and the Wear are 'off-shore' plants of multi-national companies.

In general the industries that are increasing in importance in the region are chemicals and allied industries, electrical goods, light engineering and textiles. Further expansion on Teesside is concerned with the development of North Sea oil and gas. Four drilling rigs have been built on the Tees and oil from Phillips' strikes near Norway is to be landed here.

Much of the new development involves massive capital investment but provides comparatively few jobs. For example, in the Seal Sands development, including the nuclear power station at Seaton Carew, more than £200 million is being invested at the moment, but the total number of jobs provided is something less than one thousand.

It is not simply a matter of a change of industries but of a change from a labour intensive technology to a modernized and capital intensive technology. Even the industries that are continuing and expanding in the region such as steel and chemicals are modernizing their methods so that their production can increase with fewer workers. What most new industry wants is plenty of capital, plenty of space, good port and transport facilities, but not many workers. In 1971 there were 23,000 redundancies in the region, but in spite of considerable new capital investment only 5,000 new jobs were created.

The most dramatic decrease was of course in the old traditional industries. The peak year for these industries was about 1913. In that year 225,900 men were employed in coal mining in the region. Though numbers were never as high again, the biggest drop did not occur until after the second world war. Even in 1957, there were 142,435 men employed in coal mining, but today the number is only 38,377. During that time the number of pits being worked fell from 179 in 1957 to 40 in 1974 and the present policy is towards mechanized operation concentrating on a small number of large pits situated on the east coast.

The continuing trend can be seen in the fact that between 1960 and 1970 the numbers employed in coal, steel, shipbuilding and transport fell from 258,000 to 149,000 – a loss of 40%.

We have seen how changes in industry have included changes in the location of industry and in the population pattern. Formerly, in Durham in particular, mining communities were dispersed throughout the county, but today the A1(M) motorway running through Newcastle in the north via Darlington in

the south, cuts off the declining mining areas of West Durham
from the eastern part of the region where new developments
are being concentrated. Tyneside and Wearside face competition
from Teesside, which – 'including the area from Hartlepool to
Darlington – is the area with probably the greater long term
development potential ... with ample level land, not subject to
subsidence, capable of development; capacity for considerable
port development, etc.'[5]. In the competition to get new jobs in
one area rather than another, it is easy to see how rivalries can
be sharpened.

No part of the North East remains untouched by the changes
of industry: while the villages of West Durham are cut off from
any possibility of future development, villages within travelling
distance of industry are largely taken over by commuters, a
situation in which the local people themselves tend to lose out.

As far back as 1936 the Team Valley Trading Estate in Gateshead had been set up with a view to establishing new industries
in the area and since then a number of other industrial estates
have been created. These have in some cases been linked to new
towns which have been built with the intention of creating an
image of life in the North East different from that of the old
mining villages. In 1969 a comprehensive plan, aimed to concentrate development in particular areas, was published by
the NEPC in *Outline Strategy for the North*.[6]

So much for some of the bare facts, but what about the people
concerned? The following is a sociologist's comment on County
Durham:

'Sociologically, the most distinctive features of note are the
predominance of the working class and the existence of a large
number of mining and former mining settlements dispersed over
the County ... the preponderance of the working class is most
distinctive and ... markedly different both from the large conurbations such as Newcastle upon Tyne or Greater London and
from the country as a whole.... The study of social change in
County Durham in the twentieth century is therefore primarily
the study of change in working class institutions and culture in
small and medium sized communities.'[7]

This statement is supported by the census of England and
Wales of 1961 which shows that in County Durham 77.7% of
the economically active males were manual workers and only
8.6% were in professional or managerial positions as against
65.5% manual workers and 14.3% professional and managerial
in the country as a whole.

The influence of the mining village is attested by Sid Chaplin a local writer who was brought up in the villages of Newfield and Ferryhill in County Durham:

'For many the village certainly was a prison: it became such a prison to me that in the end I just had to break out. But perhaps there was much to be learnt by that also. I broke out, only to find myself so shaped and moulded by the village that in many ways I remained inextricably its prisoner – inextricably, but willingly and for life.'

This kind of loyalty is still strong in the North East even though the small isolated community is no longer a viable unit.

At the same time, Sid Chaplin gives a typical picture of the life of women at that time: 'The very nature of the work made most women slaves, wives, daughters all. Shifts split up the family so that men would be coming in at all hours of the day, waiting for the bath-tin and the water and a woman to wash their backs ... Service was the only escape and amelioration of that black tragedy of the mining family – too many daughters.' This gives some insight into the profound changes now taking place as a variety of jobs become available to women with the introduction of new industries to the region.

The specifically working-class institutions emerged from the needs and conditions of work itself. The first need was for self-help and mutual support and various organizations were formed for this purpose. These included working men's clubs, co-operatives and above all trade unions. Even today County Durham has a larger number of working men's clubs for its population than any other part of the country – even though they now serve very different purposes. The first co-operative was formed in Hetton-le-Hole in 1825. But the most important institution was the trade union. The first miners' union which aimed to cater for both Northumberland and Durham, was formed in 1830, but this was broken by the 1831 strike. This was only the first in a succession of unions that were destroyed in similiar ways. At last a union was established in Northumberland in 1864 followed by the formation of the Durham miners' association in 1869. Nationally, Northumberland and Durham stood out for many years as being different from the rest of the country. A number of reasons have been given for this difference. Most important perhaps is their longer history, but their comparative geographical isolation must also have played a part. Nor should we see their own development within the region as a uniform matter.

The coalfield is a large one – and there were considerable

differences of outlook between the smaller mining communities in the west and the larger pits of East Durham. In the smaller communities, managers and men often lived in the same village and attended the same chapel. It was therefore easier for them to feel that they shared a common concern. The influence of Methodism combined with political Liberalism was strong and many of the union officers and later several MPs were Methodist. A number of forces were working towards a sense of unity between managers and men, but it was a view that could not be sustained when larger pits became the norm, when managers lived in different localities, and when the suffering of the depression years made it obvious that managers and men were seeking different objectives, and that progress could not be made without conflict. Though today there are still considerable differences of outlook among miners, their union is now formally linked to the Labour party and to socialist aims.

But the miners' union is only one of the main trade unions in the region. At present the chairman of the Northern Trade Unions Council is the president of the Boilermakers' Union and this is in line with the traditional importance of the craft unions in the North East. For instance in the ship-building industry: 'Despite very considerable changes which have taken place over the years a shipyard can still fairly be described as having a craft technology.... Traditionally each trade or group of related workers was organized in its own trade union.... Trade unions in the industry are powerful and control a number of important aspects of the work situation – especially recruitment to a trade through apprenticeships.'[8]

The importance of the craft unions extends throughout the whole range of engineering and many parents in the North East still pin their hopes for their sons on some kind of apprenticeship.

We have seen how in today's situation where there are fundamental changes in management and control, trade unionists like Bob, see their task as that of safeguarding the employment of their members. In this way the trade unions do not seem to have changed much and it is management that appears to constitute the biggest change. This is another matter for further study.

Industries are bigger and managers further removed from workers – the nationalization of coal and steel has increased the distance between managers and men. It is seldom possible to meet the real boss and many people find it difficult to know who their boss is. If the firm is a subsidiary of a multi-national company the chances are that 'the boss' resides in New York or even

Tokyo. Lesser managers come to the region only for a short time as a step towards promotion elsewhere. In this kind of situation it is the trade unionists who must concern themselves with the needs of local people, and who therefore often appear as the conservatives.

Of course there is a very positive side to all this, firms with sophisticated technology like ICI and others bring graduates, scientists, research workers and managers into an area that is conspicuously lacking in the particular skills they bring. Young aspiring men have come into the region like a breath of fresh air.

What I am trying to show is that there is something new here and that it is out of what we make of this newness, as it comes into contact with what is old, that a different kind of future will be created.

It is clear that there are now considerable differences of outlook in the region. I should not wish to label these as class differences for these are notoriously difficult to pin down. However, the background of the North East does seem to have produced certain important points of view that are often connected with the working class. It is important for the church's mission that these should be understood. Briefly, some of the main differences between working class and middle class outlooks have been summarized as follows:

WORKING CLASS PERSPECTIVE	MIDDLE CLASS PERSPECTIVE
General Beliefs	
The social order is divided into 'us' and 'them', those who do not have authority and those who do.	The social order is a hierarchy of differently rewarded positions; a ladder containing many rungs.
The division between 'us' and 'them' is virtually fixed, at least from the point of view of one man's life chances.	It is possible for individuals to move from one level of the hierarchy to another.
What happens to you depends a lot on luck; otherwise you have to learn to put up with things.	Those who have ability and initiative can overcome obstacles and create their own opportunities. Where a man ends up depends on what he makes of himself.

WORKING CLASS PERSPECTIVE	MIDDLE CLASS PERSPECTIVE

General Values

'We' ought to stick together and get what we can as a group. You may as well enjoy yourself while you can instead of trying to make yourself 'a cut above the rest'.	Every man ought to make the most of his capabilities and be responsible for his own welfare. You cannot expect to get anywhere in the world if you squander your time and money. 'Getting on' means making sacrifices.

Attitudes on more specific issues

(On the best job for a son) 'A trade in his hands.' 'A good steady job.'	'As good a start as you can give him.' 'A job that leads somewhere.'
(Towards people needing social assistance) 'They have been unlucky.' 'They never had a chance.' 'It could happen to any of us.'	'Many of them had the same opportunity as others who have managed well enough.' 'They are a burden on those who are trying to help themselves.'
(On trade unions) 'Trade unions are the only means workers have of protecting themselves and of improving their standard of living.'	'Trade unions have too much power in the country.' 'The unions put the interests of a section before the interests of the nation as a whole.'

Many people suggest that class differences no longer exist, but the sense of class division and the recognition that it goes much deeper than the pay packet is expressed in many local folk songs, of which the following is an example:

'The Tyne Slides By'

Salisbury Crescent and Mornington Square
Fine names for fine houses, fine people live there;
Bloomsbury Gardens and Regency Mews
Tradesmen use side entrances, no hawkers please.
Judges and generals, all fox-hunting men,
Antiques, au pair girls, villas in Spain.
Grosvenor Mansions, Victoria Close,
Calling out sweetly for Betjeman prose.

Windermere Avenues, Coniston Groves,
Neat little hutches in neat little rows,
Buttermere Crescents and Ullswater Greens,
Three pastel bedrooms for middle-class dreams.
Daddy's out teaching and Mummy will soon,
To pay back the loan on their four-door saloon,
Kiddies well-spoken, well-dressed and well-shod;
Mortgages, miseries – but pensions, thank God.

Paradise Dwellings and Colliery Rows,
Along Co-op Terrace and up Albert Road.
Inkermans, Kitcheners all round the town,
Streets fit for heroes, two up and two down,
Ypres Street, Haig Street all bronchitic black.
Bulldozers wait to begin the attack.
This year or next year or never perhaps.
New homes for heroes – Paradise Flats!
... And the Tyne slides by, the seagulls cry,
    The ships lie safe and silent at the riverside

Jack and Jill are off to serve
A sentence in the child preserve
Where iron bars confine the extra care they need.
Jack will meet his brothers there,
Those baby boilermakers fair.
And Jill will share the fate of her neglected breed,
This is where the world begins,
This is where they'll try their wings
And learn that Kings and Queens are from a different mould.
Losing as they always will,
Down the hill go Jack and Jill.
Down the river where their mams and dads were also sold.

Tim and Joy at private school
Prepared by every golden rule
So gently weaned and polished clean for finer things.
Tim is with his kith and kin
The game is tailor-made for him
And Joy will win on roundabouts as well as swings.
Tim and Joy swim with the stream,
Born to join the winning team
And mum and dad can dream of what the future brings.
Little girls and little boys,
Jacks and Jills and Tims and Joys,

Please don't make a noise, you'll spoil the scheme of things.
... And the Tyne slides by, the seagulls cry,
    The ships lie safe and silent at the riverside, etc.

Alex Glasgow

In spite of the predominance of the working class the politics
of the region were not built up on a socialist view of class conflict:
'Throughout the 1890's the sole representative of the Durham
mineworkers in Parliament was the pugnacious and sharp-tongued
John Wilson, a staunch Liberal and a determined opponent of
socialism.' Until the early part of this century the miners' leadership 'rejected socialist doctrine and fiercely resented and resisted
the concomitant idea of a new and independent working class
party'.[10]

Today Parliamentary representation of the North East is solidly
Labour with the exception of three seats – Newcastle North,
Berwick and Middlesbrough West. Local councils have more
variation but many, including places like Hebburn, still have
an almost total Labour membership, but Robert Moore suggests
that the Labour conquest of the North East was not made on
strictly ideological grounds.

This is an important point – for the struggle is not just an
ideological struggle. What we are seeing is people trying to find
ways of responding to the things that disturb their lives. And
those things almost overwhelm them.

Changes in technology, in the economy or overseas markets, put
whole communities out of work at a stroke. I am not just thinking
of Jarrow or the miners, but of firms like Reyrolles in Hebburn,
who, owing to changes in the home and overseas market have
reduced a work-force that was over 10,000 to less than 5,000
during the last five years or so.

Remoteness from national government, concentration of power
and 'know-how' in the hands of a few people locally, lack of any
political debate about fundamental issues, and the lack of rapport
between local councillors and those they represent – all contribute
to a massive indifference and cynicism about politics in general.

Loss of any sense of identity has occurred as communities break
up, traditional skills are superseded, and individuals are either
sucked into larger impersonal organizations, or thrown out of work.

Hopes that had been pinned to education as the door to
opportunity have been dashed by discovering that after all it is
a door to nowhere.

This is the situation within which people have to find ways to

respond. It is in their political response that they are trying to
come out from under this economic and industrial determinism,
and therefore the way in which people respond politically is an
important clue to how they find meaning in life.

The point that must be underlined – because it is crucial to
the whole argument of this book, is that, because these questions
are questions about meaning in life, they must be the concern
of theology. It is in the disturbances themselves that we should
look for God, it is within particular events that we come to know
God, and it is only in terms of our particular circumstances that
we can respond to God.

This means that the issues of our industrial society must be the
starting point for theology, and it means that the world 'sets the
agenda'. This does not mean that theology must take the world
on its own terms, but it does mean that theology must take the
world absolutely seriously. It is only in relation to the world's
questions that we can discover the relevance of what God has
done and will do for us and how this can be part of our living
and hoping.[11]

The gospel does not see change as a threat but as an opportunity
to break with the past and shape a new future. We do not need
to look back, but can grasp a vision of a future in which people
will be wholly themselves (not cogs in a machine) living in
community with each other and with God. It is as we share
creatively in change with the deaths and resurrections it involves
that we discover that 'the gospel has liberating power and that
it gives us the power to break out of stereotypes, to change and
become someone and something different from what we have
been – to discover and to create an open future'.

In this chapter I have given a sketch of the North East and its
changing life. I have gone into this in some detail, because I
believe this is where theology must start. It is for this reason that
I want to end the chapter by spelling out the particular ways in
which I am trying to understand the changing issues of the North
East so that theological thinking can start from them.

In the course of my job as a theological consultant I have
been keeping an eye on my involvement at various points, and
it seems to me that there are a number of recurrent questions that
come up in different forms in different places. In the same way
there appear to be recurrent Christian themes that have some
resonance. I have kept a systematic record of these things and
recently I have tried to sum this up in the table on page 69.

In the table the left hand column simply lists four main

areas of disturbance that have been identified. The second column, headed 'Social Aspect' breaks the main questions down into more particular areas of disturbance. The third column 'Personal Aspect' points to the kind of question which in fact tends to form the starting point for discussion. Many of us only notice what is happening around us when it actually affects us, so that the first question is often about the immediate effect of disturbance on our own lives. It is only when we delve more deeply into our own experience that we recognize the social and political aspects of the same question. But of course the discussion may start anywhere – on the personal, social or general level.

Looking across these three columns (without mentioning the Christian themes at this stage) the table highlights four main areas of disturbance in the North East. The first area concerns technological change and all that this means for employment and unemployment in the region where certain groups, such as the unskilled young people, suffer most. The social aspect of the question includes changes within employment – take-overs, remoteness of management and changing styles of organization. On the personal side there is insecurity and loss of identity.

The second main area is that of local government, its re-organization and the need for new forms of participation in politics, planning and in every large institution. On the personal side there is a sense of frustration, apathy and opting out. At the same time there is a recognition that old styles of authority are now inappropriate.

The third area deals with the quality of life – the environment, and cultural facilities as well as less tangible things such as the social goals and thinking embodied in the major institutions of the region.

The personal side of this emerges from the fact that work is no longer accepted as the only thing in life. So other questions become important including questions of leisure, enjoyment and meaning.

The fourth issue concerns the quality and aims of education, training and re-training. On the personal side there is concern for children's education and there are fears in many adults about whether they themselves have the ability to change and to learn new things.

The fourth column suggests some Christian themes that appear to be relevant to each point. In relation to the changes of technology there is the vision of a future which is summed up in the belief in the Kingdom of God. This gives a forward impetus to

Main Question	Social Aspect	Personal Aspect	Christian Theme
Place of work/non-work in life	Technology and change, employment/unemployment, mergers, take-overs, effects of entry to EEC, regional problems, decline of heavy industry, disadvantage of unskilled youth....	Insecurity, lack of communication. Lack of job satisfaction. People treated as machines. Need for personal identity and a balance of work and leisure. Relationships at work. Need to interpret the meaning of change.	Vision of the Kingdom of God, God's relation to the material world. Science and a Christian understanding of reality and change. Absolute value of each person as a child of God.
Politics and Participation	Local Government re-organization – cynicism about politics, corruption, pressure groups, new styles of authority and participation. Minority groups.	Sense of frustration and inability to contribute to major issues – 'us and them'. Attitudes to authority and participation, fear of conflict.	Power – its meaning and use. Service, man's place in society, criteria for a Christian critique of society, prophecy, creative conflict.
Social Goals	Quality of life – environment, 'cultural' facilities, goals of institutions and problems of change in relation to traditional thinking and practices, need for institutional flexibility and co-operation.	How do I enjoy life, find meaning in life, get some vision of new possibilities? Attitudes of 'officials'. Inability to get decisions or influence institutions.	Christian understanding of community, hope, salvation, the church, worship and social ethics.
Education	Deficiencies in education, re-training and all services, low sights and depression mentality.	Concern for children's education, need for retraining as people become redundant, fears about one's ability to change and learn new things, disgust with low standards.	The nature of man – human potentialities and the possibility of personal growth. Values for human living.

the search. Alongside this, and as a corrective to the kind of enthusiasm for change that rides roughshod over people, is the belief in the absolute value of every person as a child of God. In relation to the political questions stands the concept of power as it is understood in Christian faith. A theme for the quality of life is the Christian understanding of community and of worship, and in relation to education there is a belief in the potentialities of man as seen within Christian faith.

I have separated my comment on the Christian themes from that of the other three columns because I do not wish to suggest a direct one-to-one relationship between the Christian themes and the life questions. What I do want to do is to point to the fact that the questions that arise from life are in fact 'gospel' questions – what men and women are for, what they can hope for and what resources are available for them. If the gospel is to mean anything at all we must discover what relationship it has to life's questions – even though this is not a simple relationship of question and answer. I also want to avoid any suggestion that the gospel itself arises out of the questions of life – for I have already made clear that I believe it arises from God's action in Christ. For this reason I have found it necessary to engage in a separate piece of research from 'the other end'. This involves a study of what Christians say and what they have said in the past about their faith in God, the world, man, Christ, the Holy Spirit, the church and so on. By this means I can discover Christian themes which do not appear to have resonance today and must ask why this is so.

The table sums up a stage in the exploration and can be a means of helping people to take the next step in 'doing theology' together.

The whole research places particular questions in a larger context and can be a means of relating different explorations that are going on, and different people who are asking the same sort of questions.

The important thing about the table and this summary is that they do not come out of snap judgments about the situation, but out of careful observation of what is happening, from listening to what people say about it all and from discussing it with them. In this way, it draws together, and clarifies the main issues that require further thought and action, and can form a background to the churches' forward plans in the region.

NOTES

1. W. H. Wright, from an unpublished paper.
2. Sydney Middlebrook, *Newcastle-upon-Tyne, Its Growth and Achievements*, S. R. Publishers Ltd 1968, appendix, p. 24.
3. Sir Timothy Eden, *Durham*, Robert Hale 1952, vol. II, p. 470.
4. Middlebrook, op. cit., p. 238.
5. North Economic Planning Council, *Challenge to the Changing North*, HMSO 1966, p. 71.
6. North Economic Planning Council, *Outline Strategy for the North*, NEPC 1969.
7. Martin Bulmer, *Social Structure and Social Change in County Durham in the Twentieth Century*, University of Durham 1969.
8. Richard Brown & Peter Brannen, *Social Relations and Social Perspectives amongst Shipbuilding Workers – A Preliminary Statement*.
9. J. H. Goldthorpe & D. Lockwood, 'The Changing National Class Structure, 2', *Sociological Review*, Vol. II, no. 2, 1963.
10. Robert Moore, *Religion as a Source of Variation in Working Class Images of Society*, a paper in which he quotes from R. Gregory, *The Miners and British Politics 1906-1914*, Oxford University Press 1968.
11. See above p. 22.

VII

ONE DIVIDED CHURCH
The Churches in the North East

It was an Irishman who, when asked the way to a certain place, replied, 'If I were going there I would not start from here'. It is tempting to say the same about the church, for it has been so much shaped by the past situation that its present responses are conditioned by the responses it made in a society that no longer exists, and by a static and unchanging theology. Its buildings and manpower are where they once were needed but are not needed now! The relics of the past attempts to make new responses have fossilized into irrelevant organizations and attitudes – and the church itself is represented by a number of different denominations and sects. All in all the church is no less trapped in an ideology that has been shaped by its past than any other institution in society – industry, trade unions, politics or education. We long for the church to be free from these unnecessary restrictions, so that it can face the real life questions of today, and we believe that the gospel can liberate institutions as well as individuals. The first step towards this freedom must be to understand the situation, and, in the same way that the last chapter described the sociological context of the North East, this chapter will describe its ecclesiastical context. I shall aim to show how the church has been shaped by its past and how it is therefore hampered in its responses in the present.

The North East may only have sprung to life industrially one hundred and fifty years ago, but as far as Christian faith goes it sprang to life more than thirteen hundred years ago. In 627 Edwin, King of Northumbria was baptized at York. In 635 St Aidan became the first Bishop of Lindisfarne, having been brought from Iona by King Oswald to convert the people of Northumbria. It was in the monasteries of Monkwearmouth and Jarrow that a local boy, later known as the Venerable Bede, spent his life and achieved fame as theologian, teacher and translator of the Bible. Far from being on the periphery of life, the North East was the centre from which missionaries went out to play a major part in the re-conversion of pagan Europe. Whatever may have happened since then – invasion, despoilation, neglect – the fact remains that the church in the North East grew out of the lives of men and women who responded generously and freely to what were the actual needs of their own day.

But the situation has changed since then, and we must ask whether the church has been as free in its response to the questions of subsequent ages or whether it has been so conditioned and shaped by its past that it has not been able to make appropriate responses to new situations.

I cannot give a comprehensive history of the church, but I can sketch out enough to lead us in the direction of answers to these questions.

It was the dark ages of the ninth and tenth centuries that transformed the bishops of Durham into feudal lords with sovereign power over the Palatinate, the lands between the Tyne and the Tees with other portions of the old kingdom of Northumbria. During that time the church ceased to be represented by monks living on the lonely islands off the East coast, and the Bishop of Durham was given a place of power and wealth alongside the nobles of the North.

In this way the church became identified with certain sections of society, so that it was unable to respond to the needs of new classes created by the industrial revolution. The lasting effects of this failure are underlined by Bishop Hensley Henson when he pointed out that in the Diocese of Durham, Christianity in the mining districts is mainly Methodist, and in Tyneside mainly Roman Catholic,[1] and goes on to describe the background to this situation:

'No part of England was worse equipped than the county of Durham for sustaining the transition from an agricultural to an industrial ordering of society. The parishes were few, reflecting the sparseness of the population throughout the Middle Ages, and, indeed, through the whole period before the nineteenth century. Of the 272 parishes within the modern Diocese only 82 were in existence when that century began.... Not the most far-seeing ecclesiastical statesmen could have foreseen such a situation as that which now presents itself to the Church.

'Durham was wealthy and remote. Its wealth attracted the unfit: its remoteness protected the idle.... Upon this ill-organised and secularised Church fell suddenly the task of

providing for the spiritual needs of the great multitudes of manual
workers which the industrial development of the county was
bringing within its area. There is no need to attribute the amazing
success of the Methodist preachers to any other cause than that
which "leaps to the eyes" of the social student. Practically the
Established Church did not exist in Durham: the preachers had
the field to themselves. *"We were not Dissenters,"* said the late
John Wilson, M.P. ("the old Pilot"), himself an excellent example
of a Methodist miner, *"there was nothing for us to dissent
from"*....

'Within the Bishopric of Durham from time immemorial the
Bishop had possessed civil as well as ecclesiastical authority. In
one hand he held the pastoral staff, in the other he held the
sword; and the latter attracted more attention than the former.
It was not until 1836 that the Palatine dignity was finally severed
from the See.... To the people of Durham the Bishop has less
the aspect of a Father in God, than that of a chief Magistrate.'[2]

In this analysis of the Diocese of Durham Bishop Henson
recognized the way the past was continuing to shape the religious
and denominational patterns of his own time. What he did not
point out was that these patterns were being further re-enforced
by a particular type of theology. It was not simply a matter of the
church not having the finances or manpower to meet the demands
of industrialization, what was far more disabling was the church's
interpretation of the meaning of what was happening.

The church's theology at that time and continuing into the
present is predominantly of the Mission 'A' type. We have already
seen that this is not adequate in an industrial society. Mission 'A'
theology takes a negative view of the world – over-stressing the
facts of sin and conflict. A nostalgia for the past and a negative
attitude towards industrialization runs through a great deal of
the church's thinking, so that people look back to a time when
'Durham was a county, not of industrial towns and furnaces, but
of village greens and duckponds, of village churches and thatched
roofs' before 'those portentous triplets Science, Industry and
Democracy, first saw the light of a refined and cultivated world
which it would henceforth be their province to destroy'.[3]

Mission 'A' is not concerned with the transformation of society,
and therefore does not see the need to give serious attention to
changes in society. The three main growing points of the new
society – science, industry and democracy are seen as threats to
'A's unchanging view of the world.

What 'A' is concerned with is the salvation of individuals out of the world. Its static and propositional view of the gospel makes it impossible for 'A' to see that qualitatively new things are happening, new culture patterns are being formed and a new society is taking shape and that it is within these changes that God is working and calling men to work with him for his perfect society – the Kingdom of God.

The inevitable consequence of a view of mission which does not take seriously the church's role in the shaping of society must be that the church will itself be shaped by society. Furthermore any new responses that the church does make will be made in terms of the old patterns. The church's refusal to change its own structures in order to relate to the new structures of an industrial society, its anti-democratic and élitist understanding of leadership and the inflexibility of its theology – all these things still hamper the church's mission and limit its responses to the real questions of today.

And it is no better with the other denominations. For many years the Roman Catholic's only protection against the hostility of society was to create their own communities. Roman Catholics were brought up with Roman Catholics, went to school with Roman Catholics and mixed entirely with Roman Catholics, and in many places this is still largely true. The fact that they had to congregate together in this way and provide their own social environment has indelibly marked the religious geography of the North East. As late as 1746 there were anti-Catholic riots in Newcastle and Gateshead and it was not until 1829 that Roman Catholics were given political emancipation and could take public office.

Today there are many Roman Catholics in leading positions in the trade unions and local councils of the North East, and I have constantly been struck by the fact that many Roman Catholic workers are better able to express the relation between faith and work than members of other churches.

As Hebburn is one of the places with a concentration of Roman Catholics I arranged to talk the matter over with three members of St James' Church, Hebburn. Jim is chairman of the Hebburn District Council and an AEUW shop steward at Rey-rolle's, one of the largest employers in Hebburn, who make switchgear for the international market. Norman is also an AEUW shop steward and works at Hebburn shipyard. Both Jim and Norman live in Hebburn, a solidly working-class parish, which grew up with the shipyard which opened in 1853. Wilf, the third member of the group, lives in Gateshead but attends

St James' Church. He decided to concentrate on trade union rather than political affairs and is area representive of the sheet metal workers.

In our conversation their membership of the church appeared at first simply as a background to the place of politics and trade unions in their lives. As Jim said, 'My father would have sooner seen me become a member of the Church of England than of the Conservative party'. Their parents had lived through the depressions of the thirties and had had to stand up for themselves in what must have seemed a hostile world. Theirs were homes that knew the direct effect of political decision and indecision. Wilf said, 'My father was very bitter about the Conservatives and the war'. In addition the parents had been aware that they belonged to a church community, whose members were often at a disadvantage when it came to getting jobs.

For all three men trade union and political involvement had come about through personal involvement in some incident or other. For Norman it was the apprentices' strike of 1941-2, for Jim it was recognition of wartime fiddling in tea and chocolate by unscrupulous shop stewards, while Wilf was deeply influenced by some outstanding local men in the Labour Party.

All the time the church had been there, simply as the community to which they belonged, playing such a natural part in the development of their thinking that they seemed almost unconscious of how it had helped them.

For Jim a link was forged between work and faith through membership of the Young Christian workers, and he actually became one of its full-time organizers in the Leeds Diocese for a year until his health was affected by the constant travelling.

When he was fourteen, Wilf joined discussion and educational classes run by the Catholic Young Men's Society. Later he went on to the Catholic Social Guild which studies the nature of Christian social obligation in a more sustained way, and from this he was awarded a two-year grant to study politics and economics at the Catholic Worker's College in Oxford.

It was clear that these educational opportunities played a major part in forming their thinking. The fact that many working men belong to the church and many of the priests are themselves sons of working men gives a natural setting for their continuing development.

This is one side of the story, an outward going response to the needs of society in line with the concern for social justice that was given new impetus by Vatican II. But Roman Catholics themselves would be the first to recognize that there is another side to things and that all that was negative in the past continues to influence the church towards isolationism and inflexibility. Rather than being concerned with the transformation of the world, many Roman Catholics still think of the church as their world.

John Wesley and his followers did respond creatively to the urgency of the needs of the new industrial workers.

Bishop Henson pointed out that the Church of England simply did not exist in the new mining areas of Durham at the time of industrialization, and that the field was left open to the Wesleyans and later to the Primitive Methodists. Just how different their approach was can be seen from a description of John Wesley as he appeared during his numerous visits to the region:

'Here was no placid, Christian gentleman, but a thunderbolt of God.... This was a prophet, an enthusiast, a man possessed and possessing, who inspired and shook and captured and captivated, and drove his hearers into physical ecstasies and agonies at his feet.'[4]

There can be no doubt that Methodism had a remarkable influence at a critical time in the life of the area. But that was two hundred years ago – and we must now ask how far the Methodists too have become prisoners of their past, how far they have the kind of theology that enables them to continue to shape society rather than being shaped by it.

Robert Moore, who has done some detailed sociological studies of the influence of Methodism among Durham miners, points out that most statements about the influence of Methodism are too general and do not allow for the fact that a number of different influences and circumstances came together at a particular time to produce certain results and that the pattern has changed from one generation to the next. He remarks that more work must be done before we can make any general statement. What follows is based on his own studies and comments.[5]

In a study of four small villages in West Durham, whose total population never exceeded 9,000, he shows the extent to which Methodists occupied positions in the union leadership between the early 1870s and the first world war. 'There were long periods in the villages when all the key union posts were held by Methodists.... This apparent dominance of the Methodists had been virtually universal in the earlier years. It was also a *collective* exercise of power by Methodism, for all the key figures in the local unions interacted in the chapels and were bound to other Methodists through kinship and common activities.

'An understanding of Methodism is one of the keys to understanding the nature of the local union leadership. This can best
be explicated by asking two questions: firstly, how did the
Methodist see himself and secondly what was the Methodist's
understanding of social and industrial relations? ...

'The sense of being a saved man, and a man of some ethical
standing provided something of the basis of trade union morality
also. According to MacIntyre, union morality rests on the view
that a man is "essentially equal to those who claim superiority
over him, and that in knowing that he is equal to them he has
his chief weapon against them". The Methodist could stand face
to face with the owner or the managers in a self-assured and
dignified way. He expected to be respected by management.

'The Methodist's idea of society was partly bound up with the
idea of the "calling".... Thus the Methodist miner was called
to be a good miner, but by implication the coal owner was also
called to be a good coal owner. Each has his place in God's plan
and the overall social arrangements between men were not
questioned in any fundamental way.'

The study goes on to show how a number of changes have led
to a decline in Methodist influence. Methodism had never had the
same strength in the larger pits of East Durham as it had in the
smaller communities of West Durham. Now the large pits of
the East developed while the smaller pits closed down. Although
many miners moved to the East, another factor was at work, that
was the social aspirations of Methodist parents, which reduced
the recruitment of Methodists to the pits.

'Notions of class and class politics did not begin to gain real
currency in the villages until the outbreak of unmistakable and
very bitter class warfare in the 1920s.' Then the Methodist view
of society no longer fitted the facts. 'The historical links between
Methodism, Liberalism and the union were broken and with this
break the influence of the Methodists in politics and industrial
affairs waned. The tight base of union, lodge, chapel, co-op, and
Liberal party sponsorship had been destroyed. The Labour
Party emerged as a specifically political institution and the
chapels remained in effect, as wholly religious organisations.'
This was the strongest reason for the decline of Methodist influence, but the question it raises is not simply a question for
Methodists but for us all. How can we find meaning in political
events?

There are of course still many Methodists holding office in
trade unions and government. Ernest Armstrong, Labour MP

for West Durham, represents much that is best in Methodism. Lately I talked with a councillor representing one of the Easington parishes, in which there are at present a number of Methodist councillors. He is a lay preacher and a keen member of his own church at Blackhall. It is people like this who must help to answer our question.

But trade unionism and politics are only a part of Methodism. Ernie was brought up in Stillington where his father was a blast-furnaceman. The family were such strict Methodists that Ernie's father would not even shave on a Sunday. 'Sunday was torture', said Ernie – 'The day was spent in chapel beginning with Sunday school in the morning. There was no humanity in it all – and the few families that attended chapel were more than ready to scratch each others eyes out. It was like a strait jacket – but I was searching for abundant life.' Even today, having been a lay preacher for many years, Ernie feels at odds with traditional Methodists who are prepared to take it all 'from the book'.

'The crude dogmatism and cruder worship which gave strength to the earlier Methodists'[6] may have served the first generation of industrial workers, but they are not appropriate responses for today.

We are forced to the conclusion that in one way or another the whole church is trapped in its past so that if people like Ernie are to respond to life as it is today, they must escape.

Change

This does not say that the church is not changing, and in spite of all I have said about being trapped, changes are taking place. In this section I describe three examples of change in the church and ask how far these are real responses to real questions or on the other hand how far they are shaped by the present existence of the church and its past responses. The first two examples are taken from the Church of England, but I want to make clear that I believe all the churches are in the same predicament.

(a) New forms of ministry

The strength of the Church of England has been in the quality and devotion of its parish clergy. In pre-industrial society life was lived in more or less self-contained communities and the parish priest could minister to people in all aspects of their lives. Industrialization changed the pattern of society – so that life is now lived in a number of different communities and institutions. If it is to face the questions of today the church also needs a new structure. But the church has not seen things that way. It has realized that something is wrong, and that it has lost much of its influence and touch with people, but it has not realized why this is so. Instead of making basic changes, it has therefore made just enough change to enable it to go on answering the old questions in some new settings. Consequently we have the odd situation in which the church has set up new forms of ministry, but is asking them to do the old things, and is sucking them back into the old patterns.

Owing to its greater financial resources and the relative autonomy of the diocesan bishops, the Church of England has been in a better position than most other churches to set up new forms of ministry. In the Diocese of Durham, for instance, there is a regular meeting of representatives of such ministers with the bishop. This meeting became necessary as many of them had no recognized place in the church's structure. The meeting includes two types of minister – those with a service function such as the education team, planning officer, stewardship officer and theological consultant, and secondly those with responsibility for a particular sector of society – such as industrial mission, social responsibility, hospital chaplain, arts and recreation. It is this latter group that I want to discuss at this juncture. This group of ministries was pioneered by industrial mission and the others follow the same general principles, so I shall take industrial mission as my example.

Industrial mission is clearly of great importance in industrial society, and it is a form of ministry that is now world wide. In the North East there are two industrial missions – one in the North, the Northumberland and North Durham Industrial Mission, and one in the South, the Teesside Industrial Mission.

We have already seen that there are two dimensions of mission.[7] The first is expansion, which is not primarily a geographical or numerical affair, but means that the church must continually enter areas where Christ is not explicitly acknowledged. In entering industry the church enters one of the most secularized areas of modern life. The second dimension is penetration – which means getting inside the meaning of what is happening, so that issues are clearly understood and faced. This need for penetration springs from a particular theological understanding that sees the close relation of life and faith. This shows why it is more important to establish deep, long-term relationships with a few representative firms, than to attempt an overall coverage, a point that is missed by those who continue to work to a different theological understanding and to the old model of individual pastoral care within each parish.

It is the nature of the task that has given industrial mission its specific characteristics. First of all a ministry in industry demands a perspective which starts from a concern with the world rather than with the church. Its starting point must be the way people feel about their jobs, the relationships between people and groups in industry and so on.

The second characteristic is ecumenism. A concern with the whole world must be the concern of the whole church. For this reason industrial mission must create ecumenical structures. The two industrial missions of the North East straddle diocesan boundaries, include chaplains of different denominations and have ecumenical management committees.

The third and perhaps the most important characteristic is that lay people, in their secular roles, are seen to be the chief agents of God's work. In industry the minister is always on someone else's pitch – it is the lay person who is the 'expert' while the minister is the 'layman'. Nothing can be done unless those who actually work in the firm give it their support and the minister cannot even get into the firm unless he is invited. Mission in industry is primarily a matter for lay people and the minister's role is that of helper. Finally the communication of Christian faith can only take place in relation to the actual situation and its needs. To start from this point and to develop an awareness of the relevance of Christian faith requires specific skills and a very different style of theology from what is usually taught or practised.

These characteristics are common to all the 'sector' ministries. I believe that they are relevant to the whole church. But because these ministries were set up without any real understanding of their purpose, the result has been all kinds of problems and tensions.

First, there are the organizational problems. The church's whole structure is based on the parochial ministry as the norm. There is no place for 'sector' ministries, and no way for them to relate to the parochial ministry. In fact, as each 'sector' represents an *ad hoc* response to a specific need, there is no way for them to relate to each other. So there is not only tension and suspicion between parochial and sector ministries but also between the sectors themselves.

Secondly, there are financial problems. The church has limited resources and it is clear that growth in one form of ministry must mean decline in another form.

Behind these problems is an instinctive feeling that the sectors present a threat to the old ways. This has led to various reactions: from the attempt to contain the problem by making the new ministries into self-contained departments on the periphery of the church's life; to the attempt to destroy them by denigration or cutting off funds. One thing that cannot be done, however, is to ignore the problem hoping it will go away, for the tensions we have mentioned are only symptoms of the much deeper cleavage within the church, which is the cleavage between different theologies of mission. Nor is this simply a difference between sector and parochial clergy, but a difference that cuts through the whole church.

It is not simply a matter of two groups giving different answers to the same question, but of two groups addressing themselves to two completely different questions. One group is asking questions about the world, while the other is asking questions about the church. One group seeks for God's will within the changes of the world, the other seeks God's will in spite of the changes of the world. One group aims at the transformation of society, the other aims at the transformation of the individual by rescuing him out of society.

(b) Team ministries

If sector ministries raise more problems than they answer perhaps it is easier to make modifications to the parochial structure itself. One of the main changes taking place within the parochial system is the introduction of team ministries and in the last few years a number have been created in this area.

For instance, a team ministry for the whole town of Sunderland was the chief proposal made by a commission set up by the Bishop of Durham with the following terms of reference:

'To enquire into the place of the Church in the County Borough of Sunderland and to make recommendations for its future contribution to the life and welfare of the community, its civic, industrial and social life, taking account of the changing patterns of ministry, the present assets and organisations of the Church, its concern for education at all levels, and the possible re-organisation of Deanery and parochial boundaries.'

The first thing we notice about these terms of reference and about the report itself is that the question is being understood in terms of the present structure of the church rather than in terms

of the actual questions of society. The chairman of the commission was a retired civil servant, who made it clear that she
saw her task as a purely administrative one. The particular
sub-committee of which I was a member tried to raise the fundamental theological questions of meaning and purpose, but they
were disallowed.

In this case team ministry was seen as no more than a convenient adaptation of the traditional patterns of the church's
life. The change was prompted by financial and manpower
difficulties within the church with the needs of the community
as only a secondary consideration.

There are of course people who see teams as a genuine way
of engaging more effectively with an increasingly complex
environment. When this is the case the implications are so far
reaching that the same kind of tensions are bound to arise as
in the case of sector ministries. For what is happening is that
two views of mission are coming into conflict.

The theological differences do not only involve the seriousness
with which society is viewed, but also include the important issue
of leadership and authority. The old model of society with which
the church was closely affiliated saw leadership in terms of an
élite and reacted strongly against the rise of democracy. This is
still the normal model of leadership within the church and it is
re-enforced by a Mission 'A' style of theology, which sees the
clergyman's job as safeguarding and handing on an authoritative
and fixed gospel. In this view the authority of the church is
vested in a hierarchical ministry of a pyramid type with bishops
at the top, incumbents next, followed by junior clergy and finally
lay people at the bottom.

The crisis in authority and leadership is one of the fundamental
disturbances of our society. The young person at school or college,
the worker at work, the ratepayer in the local community are all
beginning to recognize that they must become active participants
in their own worlds in order to become mature human beings.
The crisis is about the humanization of society but if the church
is to make any contribution it must consider whether humanization is being furthered in its own structures of authority and
leadership. The challenge is for a much greater mutuality of
working together, and the church's own style must change in
order to form a proper base for its work in the world. It cannot
help forward human co-operation in society if it is not learning
what this means in its own life. Unfortunately the church's
theology hampers its response to this challenge. Theology of the

Mission 'A' type proposes that the church has different rules from any other institution, and that priesthood carries with it an exclusive right to leadership. I have tried to show that the gospel has an authority of its own, but that the gospel can never be the possession of any one person or group. Because the gospel is something that is shared, it demands an organic unity in the church. This means that clergy must learn to trust each other and work together. Lay people must also work together. Above all, clergy and laity must learn to work together as equals – mutually giving and receiving from each other. Only in this way will the church become the church instead of just being the parson.

(c) Ecumenism

A major ecumenical change in the North East has been the start of the North East Ecumenical Group, which is a regular meeting of church leaders throughout the region. The meeting includes the Bishops of Newcastle and Durham and the suffragan Bishop of Whitby, who has episcopal oversight in Teesside, the auxiliary Bishop of the Roman Catholic Diocese of Hexham and Newcastle, the Chairmen of the Methodist districts of Newcastle and Darlington, representatives of the Baptists, the United Reformed Church and the Salvation Army, together with the respective ecumenical officers. Officially the meeting has no executive powers, but in fact it has initiated several projects and has the potential to fulfil an obvious need for unity in the work of the church in the region.

This is a great step forward, but there are some real problems to be faced. The first is that everything the group wishes to do must be processed through the denominational structures. This has resulted in misunderstandings, short circuiting, and crossed wires. Furthermore the group has no back-up services either of a research and theological kind or of an executive kind – apart from a clerical secretary for whom this has to be one job among many. It cannot be expected that a group of such busy people could initiate and carry out the fundamental policies they might like.

For instance, the Ecumenical Social Responsibility group they set up with representatives from all parts of the region only had a short life because it could not even keep a representative committee together, let alone find the resources for implementing any plans it might come up with. While the plans for Action North East, which aimed to involve the whole region in ongoing mission caused immense misunderstandings at the denominational and local level. One cause of this was the fact that the presentation did not take full enough account of the various theological points of view so that fundamental questions about aim remained unanswered and the enterprise failed to convey vision or to win sufficient backing. As a result it has never really got off the ground.

What we have here is another instance of a reaction to change that is being made within the terms of the old patterns of church life.

These three examples show that changes are taking place in the churches, but that they are being made in response to problems that face the church not those that face society. In the past the church made certain responses – the reasons for these responses have long since ceased to obtain, but the church goes on trying to do what it has done in the past.

No relevant change can take place until we begin to do theology together in the ways I have described. This means sharing in the struggle to find meaning in life. It means taking life absolutely seriously – knowing that it is in people and events in the present that God reveals himself to us, and that it is in terms of our present situation that we must respond.

Theology means looking at life in the light of the gospel. When we dare to do this we find that even bigger changes are demanded of us than we had imagined. Theology is not an abstract exercise but asks about the meaning of action and clarifies new directions. This means it has practical consequences. The last part of this book will be concerned with what those practical consequences are: the church must be in touch with the issues of society: the church must enable a revolution of the laity to take place: the church must draw out and use the skills of all sorts of people. All this can only be achieved by co-operation. The church is first and foremost people, and its members must support each other and encourage each other to face the kind of change that will create a different future.

Together we can dare to do things that seem impossible and frightening while we try to act in isolation. It is as we 'do theology' together that we are set free for mission, instead of concentrating all our energies on trying to hold on to what we already have. Mission means extending into life and exploring all that God is now offering to us in Christ.

Many things must happen outside the church, but this is not to say that the church is to be discarded. None of these things will happen unless there is a church, and it is essential that it should be liberated from the unnecessary impediments of the past and its own internal debates so that it can plunge into life and find meaning there.

NOTES

1. *Relative Strength of the Denominations on Tyneside in 1928*
Figures taken from Henry A. Mess, *Industrial Tyneside*, Ernest Benn Ltd, 1928. It is difficult to get comparable statistics as each denomination calculates its membership in a different way, and the denominational boundaries differ.

Church of England 70% of children born on Tyneside were baptized in the Church of England. 9% of the population over 18 years of age were on the electoral rolls (total 46,658).

Roman Catholic (Figures cover the Diocese of Hexham and Newcastle, i.e. Northumberland and Durham Counties, and refer to 1925). 18% of the children born in the area were baptized in the Roman Catholic Church. 9.7% of the total population were taken to be members of the Roman Catholic Church. In Tyneside 12.5% of the population were taken to be members of the Roman Catholic Church. In some areas this was considerably higher, especially in Jarrow, Hebburn and Blaydon. This means the Roman Catholic Church was the strongest on Tyneside.

Presbyterian 2% of the adult population of Tyneside were communicant members of the Presbyterian Church – a considerably higher proportion than in other parts of the country.

Methodist Primitive, United and Wesleyan Methodists together were over 5% of Tyneside's population. Their Sunday schools were even stronger, and at that time there was a rise in Methodist membership on Tyneside as people came from the country to live in the city and suburbs.

Salvation Army probably came next, while *Baptists* and *Congregationalists* had fairly small numbers. In addition there were other groups and missions and several Jewish synagogues.

2. H. Hensley Henson, *Retrospect of an Unimportant Life*, Oxford University Press 1943, vol. II, pp. 79-80.

3. Sir Timothy Eden, *Durham*, Robert Hale 1952, vol. II, pp. 287, 289.

4. Op. cit., p. 391.

5. Robert Moore, *Religion as a Source of Variation in Working Class Images of Society*. See also Robert Moore, *Pitmen, Preachers and Politics*, Cambridge University Press 1974.

6. Henson, op. cit., vol. II, p. 80.

7. See above p. 39.

THE CONSEQUENCES

VIII

RAISING THE ISSUES
God the Disturber

The goal of wholeness through the process of disturbance may sound contradictory but it fits the facts of life and of faith.

The facts of life are disturbing – technological and economic growth have led to an increased gap between rich and poor and not to human wellbeing; material resources have not increased with demand but are running out; world population is outstripping food production; industrial development increases and so does industrial unrest; the smaller the world becomes the greater are its tensions; the rising aspirations of the majority go hand in hand with the concentration of power in the minority; as knowledge increases, the power to control slips away; efficiency makes less and less sense because the meaning and purpose of the whole thing has been lost. Change is the only constant and we long for at least one point where there is no change.

Some people look for stability in the church only to find that the gospel does not promise stillness but even more disturbance:

'And there will be signs in sun, moon and stars, and upon the earth distress of nations in perplexity at the roaring of the sea and the waves, men fainting with fear and foreboding of what is coming to the world; for the powers of heaven will be shaken' (Luke 21.25-26).

Does this mean that God himself is the disturber?

All through this book I have shown that there are different ways of understanding Christian faith. There will therefore be different interpretations of and responses to these disturbances. On the one hand those who, with Mission 'A' put their emphasis on sin and the negative factors in the world will see the disturbances as a threat to their own identity and to the church and its mission. To them the upsurge of aspiration and energies throughout the world will appear to have nothing in common with Christian goals, but will seem to threaten the peace and harmony of the world. They look back to more settled times when the church counted for something and their response will be to draw closer together to protect the gospel from being lost in an uncomprehending world.

On the other hand there is the point of view that I have put forward in this book, which is my own understanding of events. We should expect to find God in the disturbances for we believe that it is in and through people and events in the world that God makes himself known. God is concerned with change and he is at work to transform the whole world, and to unite all things in Christ. If, in the meantime, the acceptance of something less hinders the drive towards wholeness, God the disturber, will not hesitate to break it up. Our response to this should not be fear but expectation.

This means that the first task for Christians is to look for God in and through the things that are disturbing people in the world, and to see these things, not as threats, but as growing points. In this chapter we shall see what this means today, what responses should be made and what action should be taken by the church.

It may help to look at some examples from the many areas of disturbance in life today. Education is one such area where everything is being shaken up. I have recently talked with a number of lecturers in colleges of education and technical colleges who face radical plans for reorganization into consortiums of one kind or another. Some of them are struggling to get an overall picture of what is happening but for the most part they can only see what is happening in their own patch – and that is puzzling enough. The questions that are uppermost are: 'Where will I fit into the new organization?' 'Who will I be working with?' 'How much control will I have over my own activities?' 'Will the special identity of my college be preserved?' 'Which way should I jump?' Major changes of this kind threaten the jobs and identity of the people involved and these questions must be faced. But some people are searching for the meaning of it all: 'Will the changes improve the quality of education?' 'Will the students benefit?' and 'What is the overall vision within which these changes make sense?' In all this turmoil the one thing that should be apparent to us is that education as it is simply will not do.

Another example concerns the trade unions. The trade unions

were formed in response to the particular needs of the first centuries of industrialization in this country. Their objective was to
bind together the workers in particular crafts or industries to
protect their interests in the face of unbridled exploitation. Today
changes in technology have changed the whole picture. An
increase in the number of general and white collar workers has
changed the position of the craft unions and threatened their
special identity. Workers must now be able to move from one job
to another in which they must learn completely new skills. The
identity of all unions is confused and there are considerable
tensions between unions. We have already seen the kind of
problem that technological change raises for trade unionists like
Bob, an AEUW convenor, who was the only person concerned
when the needs of the workers were threatened by changes in his
firm. Change can be utterly ruthless, as workers know to their
cost, and some sort of trade unions are needed. People like Bob
realize that what is happening to them is only part of much bigger
changes in industry. They need some understanding of where
it is all going so that they can join together in new ways and take
new initiatives. But what is clear is that, like education, trade
unions, as they are simply will not do.

Neither education, industry or any other institution really
understands itself or what is happening to it in this changing
situation. But we have already seen in chapter V from the lists
of questions produced by secular groups that many people are
asking serious questions about the meaning of what is happening
in the economy, in science and technology, in race relations and
many other areas of human life. Some people may catch a glimpse
of the truth, but they are not able to see enough to be able to
see things whole. It is not, therefore, surprising that the typical
response of the individual is fear for his own identity, and of the
institution renewed efforts for its own self-preservation.

But Christians should not see disturbance as threats but as
growing points, and it is where disturbance is most apparent
that we should look for God, and be ready to respond to the new
opportunities he is offering to us in and through the upsets. This
is the way he is re-creating and transforming the whole world.
The Christian attitude will not be one of 'fainting with fear and
with foreboding of what is coming on the world' for he will
take to heart the words that follow this passage in St Luke's
gospel:

'And then they will see the Son of Man coming on a cloud
with power and great glory. Now when these things begin to take

place, look up and raise your heads, because your redemption is drawing near' (Luke 21.26-28).

It is possible that this passage does not convey the meaning I intend, for it has been used to support an outdated world view and to suggest that God works from outside the world in an arbitrary way rather than from within the world continuously. For this reason I will quote a passage from Teilhard de Chardin, the great French scientist and theologian, who spent his life thinking through the meaning of God's activity in the world in relation to a modern scientific world view:

'Expectation – anxious, collective and operative expectation of an end of the world, that is to say of an issue for the world – that is perhaps the supreme christian function and the most distinctive characteristic of our religion.

'Historically speaking, that expectation has never ceased to guide the progress of our faith like a torch. The Israelites were constantly expectant, and the first Christians too. Christmas, which might have been thought to turn our gaze towards the past, has only fixed it further in the future. The Messiah, who appeared for a moment in our midst, only allowed himself to be seen and touched for a moment before vanishing once again, more luminous and ineffable than ever, into the depths of the future. He came. Yet now we must expect him – no longer a small chosen group among us, but all men – once again and more than ever. The Lord Jesus will only come soon if we ardently expect him. It is the accumulation of desires that should cause the Pleroma to burst upon us.

'Successors to Israel, we Christians have been charged with keeping the flame of desire ever alive in the world.'[1]

Teilhard makes it clear that Christians should see in the disturbances and issues of life God's unfailing drive towards a final issue – the summing up of all things in Christ – the *pleroma*. Therefore, in spite of our understandable apprehensions, we should look for God in the things that break up what is settled and comfortable.

In the light of this vision the first job of Christians and of the church is to know what the real issues are and to be in touch with the people and areas of life where disturbance is greatest. In order to do this the church must be close enough to the different areas of life to be able to identify the crucial issues and to distinguish them from what is merely 'newsworthy'. It must have the kind of continuing relationship which will make it possible to fulfil its own role in relation to these issues, and it must be clear what that role is.

At this point I want to be absolutely explicit about the steps that I believe must be taken by the church if it is to fulfil its distinctive function in our own time.

1. First of all, the significance of lay people in their secular roles must be grasped. When we understand 'the church' as 'the people' it is not difficult to see that the church is already more or less involved in the main areas of life by reason of the fact that there are Christian teachers, trade unionists, managers, house-wives, local councillors, members of parliament, scientists and so on. They are at the points of tension and disturbance whether they like it or not, because that is where their jobs and daily occupations put them. This is absolutely crucial for our under-standing of the church and its function in an industrial society. They are where they are in order to be leaven, salt, interpreters and catalysts in the fulfilment of God's purposes in the world.

2. But the tragedy is that lay people do not see it this way, for the fact is that Christians are even more puzzled than other people by the changes and disturbances of life. The reason for their added bewilderment is that they have separated faith and life and do not look for God's action in the whole of life. This was evident in the narrow concerns of Christian groups in comparison with the more fundamental concerns of the secular groups mentioned in chapter V. There is not much point in saying that Christians are in touch with life, if they are unable to fulfil their calling to bring insight from the gospel to their daily life. The one most urgent task for the church is to help lay people under-stand how faith and life go together. This means helping them to do theology in the way I have described – thinking through the meaning of life and faith as a whole not as two separate things. I continually come up against the assumption that theology is 'good' for some people – the 'experts' and the 'intellectuals' but not for others – the 'ordinary' lay people. What must be made plain is that theology is absolutely essential for everyone. The church cannot be true to its function in the world if its members don't understand 'who' they are and 'what' they are meant to be doing. This is what theology is about. No one should be in doubt about the revolution that would result from doing theology in this way. At present the powers and possibilities of the laity are still 'in captivity; [they] exist as frozen credits and dead capital'[2] but once they are released there will be no holding them. This revolution of the laity is so central to the changes that must

take place in the church that I shall discuss it more fully in the next chapter.

Before leaving the subject, however, I want to underline the urgency of helping lay people link faith and life by describing the kind of thing that is at present happening in the church synods.

During the 1973-4 fuel crisis one synod actually got round to discussing the subject: 'The Current Crisis – What should Christians do?' Some of the contributions to the discussion showed a great deal of understanding, but many of them simply brought out the confusion that exists in Christian thinking about life and faith.

Before the debate started one man proposed that it should not take place at all. His reasons were that: the subject was too complex for Christians to tackle: disagreement would mean that there could be no clear policy for action: because members belonged to different political parties the debate would cause dissension in the church: and synod time should not be used for educational purposes. A second speaker, who is a trade union official, was naïve enough to say he confronted all problems with the simple statement, 'I am a Christian'. He seemed to think this statement released him from the responsibility of further thought.

A third member, who is a company director, linked the crisis with what he saw as a softening of national character and urged the need for more discipline and sense of the duty of working for a living!

The tragedy is that the church is producing this kind of confusion in the minds of people, who otherwise would have something of value to contribute from their experience. Lay people like this must be helped to do theology together, so that theology rather than their position in society moulds their understanding of the gospel. If this is to be done there must be trained theologians who can help them to do it. This is a duty that the church owes to its members.

3. My emphasis on the need to take the world and its affairs absolutely seriously may have suggested that I do not attach much importance to the church. On the contrary, just the opposite is true, for I believe it is absolutely essential for the church to have its own recognizable identity. I see no point in swinging from one extreme of the pendulum, where the church is totally absorbed in itself, to the other extreme where it loses any separate identity by being totally absorbed in the world.

The church's identity comes from the gospel – that is its

identification with Christ and the way of Christ. In common with other institutions it has a two-fold task – an external task in relation to the world, and an internal task in relation to its own life. These two jobs are inter-related and must go on at the same time. Christians cannot sort themselves out and then get involved in the world – for 'it is in giving that we receive', and there must be a balance so that the 'inward' and 'outward' journeys help each other. We have seen that the church's job in the world consists of moving forwards, making new responses to new situations, with the expectation that the issues of our time are significant for the final issue for the whole world. This hope can only be maintained if the church understands the gospel in the light of the belief that God is active in the world.

But the church does not only point to the future, it should also demonstrate the present possibilities of life. The reality that is dimly sensed in the hopes and struggles of many people should to some extent already be visible in the life of the church. It should be a sign of the quality of community that all humanity is intended to enjoy. This means that the church must become the kind of body in which the members really do help each other to grow, contribute and open out. We all know that it is not what it should be and we must face the fact that for the church or any part of it to approach this ideal means a long and painful slog. But there is no use for salt that has lost its savour, and a church that has lost its own identity has nothing to contribute to the issues of the world.

4. Lay people in isolation, scattered throughout society can make little impact on the issues of society. There must be some means by which those who have similar concerns can work together. A practical approach that has been developed is that of frontier groups:

'The Frontier group has proved to be an invaluable tool of mission. A frontier exists wherever there are differences, barriers, or conflicts between groups – managers and men; conservatives and communists; black and white; police and offenders; managers and men in industry and teachers, youth employment officers and youth workers; doctors, nurses, social workers and patients; college staffs and students; evangelicals and radicals; clergy and laity; planners and planned for; etc. Any frontier may become a place of meeting and exchange of insights and experience. It can lead to reconciliation and creative progress.

'Frontier groups arise when someone who has become aware of a problem shared by a number of people and organisations who are unable or unwilling to tackle it, raises enough skill to get them together. This is an enabling role. These groups last as long as the issue remains real and then disband, perhaps or re-form on something else. They are not recruiting grounds for any ideology or organisation, though deeply held convictions will naturally be voiced. Members normally take action not through the Frontier group itself but in the appropriate institutions from which they come.

'Theologically, they are ways of expressing the creative, reconciling love of God within the secular organisations of His world.'[3]

I have experience of successful frontier groups that have looked at all sorts of issues: those raised by road development, the need for play areas, questions that concern head teachers and industrial employers, clergy and local councillors, shop stewards' training and so on. These have been started in different ways and by different people – including lay people, congregations, or members of a congregation, industrial chaplains and so on.

One of the most interesting frontier groups I have been involved in was set up by two laymen to consider the problems of semi-rural areas on the borders of large conurbations.

They had gained some understanding of what a frontier group is at a week-end consultation on urban ministry set up by the Teesside Council of Churches for lay people from congregations in the area. Both of them lived in different parts of East Cleveland, an area to the south of the County Borough of Teesside. One of them was an estate agent, a member of the Church of England and a Conservative; the other was a research worker in the British Steel Corporation, a Methodist and a Labour councillor in the North Riding. The common concern that brought them together was the effects on their area of a development of the conurbation of Teesside. They could not at this stage see exactly what the problems were, but they knew that there were matters that needed looking at. They therefore invited about thirty people to meet for a week-end. These included farmers, estate agents, shopkeepers, local councillors, teachers, students, and the county planning officer.

Much of the week-end was spent in group discussion during which two main problems were identified. The first was the need for more participation in planning and the two councillors undertook to form a continuing group, which would not be confined to those present, to think through the kind of questions that should be put to the county survey and plan when it appeared. At the same time they would make some note of the general things that would help participation in planning to become more than a slogan.

The other problem concerned the lack of leisure facilities in the area. A young teacher took the lead in setting up a continuing group, which has in fact been instrumental in establishing an arts centre in the area.

My role in this group was as theological consultant, and I saw this as helping the members to work through initial barriers that inhibited free exchange between them, helping them to clarify the key issues and encouraging them to go forward in a cooperative way.

I believed that they needed to gain some common understanding of their situation and the issues they faced, if they were to see any relevance in the gospel. Among this group of eminently practical people there was a good deal of cynicism about the usual role of the church and they needed to be helped towards a new understanding of its true function in relation to their own needs. The possibility of gaining this new understanding was almost destroyed by one woman who was a staunch church member, coming in late on the Sunday morning advertising the fact that she was the only member who had been to church. Her action did a great deal of harm for it suggested that she had a 'package' answer to the questions that were concerning the group, and she was setting herself over against the other members instead of working with them in the search for understanding. It is essential in frontier situations of this kind that church members free themselves from the kind of anxieties that impel them to want to 'preach' at others.

5. If the church really takes lay people in their secular roles seriously there will be implications for the work of the clergy, for the ministry of the clergy cannot be entirely separated from that of lay people. Clergy must also be in touch with the issues of the world, and not simply shout encouragement from the stands. At present nearly all the clergy are deployed in the residential areas of life and only a few have been appointed to be where people work, where they exercise political responsibility, where they enjoy leisure and culture and so on.

Even where 'extra-parochial' ministers have been appointed, the church has little understanding of the significance of these appointments for its whole life.

These ministers are not trying to do the lay person's job for him, but to get alongside people in order to help them identify the issues from within the situation. For instance, a social responsibility officer, spending a good deal of time with local politicians, can get inside the particular ways in which problems about the use of power and the handling of conflict are being felt by the people concerned. Someone working with the police discovers the way in which police are having to cope with changes in the law. Each one has to achieve some sort of continuing relationship with the institutions concerned in order to be able to build up the necessary relationships. An industrial chaplain, for instance, will negotiate a relationship with one or two firms and will base his work on regular visits to them. In no case are the real issues clear from outside so it is always a matter of patient learning and gaining trust if the minister is to get a true perspective on the meaning of life and how it is experienced by people in his particular field of operation. Things that are often talked about in vague generalizations take on a different dimension when they are met in concrete situations. For instance there is a myth that 'women like repetitive jobs' and I was able to test this out in conversation with a group in an electronics factory that employs a large number of women, who are making telephone switchgear.

Audrey, who is an inspector, asserted, 'The jobs here are interesting and I have to be on the spot all the time.' She was backed up by Eva, another inspector, who said, 'It takes seventeen weeks to train anyone to work in my section.' But Phoebe who works on the frames for the switchgear disagreed with them and said, 'Some of the jobs are boring and I for one would like more change.' Norman summed it up by saying, 'Women don't like boring jobs, but they're the only people who will do them.'

That may be an unexceptional conversation but at least it confronts us with the actual situation, and shows that there is an issue about the kind of satisfaction people get or do not get in their work, and it is a starting point for further exploration. The chaplain in this particular works is in fact doing a good deal of exploration and has discussed this with people at all levels. He has been fortunate in discovering a manager who is equally concerned with the question, and this has led to a series of consultations in the firm on what must be done to increase job satisfaction.

Where does the gospel come into all this? In terms of talking about God – not at all, but in terms of becoming more open to the reality of God – the gospel is at the heart of what is happening. For in the question of job satisfaction one of the main issues of the meaning of life is being focussed and people are beginning

to face it together. In this way their attention is being directed
to where God is to be met – in life – not in some abstract realm
apart from life. At the same time a prevalent idea, that springs
from the Mission 'A' line of thought is being corrected – the
concern with job satisfaction suggests that work, instead of being
a hard discipline to prepare us for another world, should be
fulfilling.

At this point we must notice what is happening rather than
what is being said. Of course, some reflection is going on all
the time, people talk about what is happening, notice changes in
the situation, discover that things can be changed, and notice
the way people and groups react both positively and negatively –
a matter which opens up further questions about human nature
itself, which is after all one of the perennial theological questions.

What I want to make clear is that life itself raises questions
of meaning and we do not have to try to impose some 'teaching'
from outside. God is to be met within the situation and what we
have to do is to help people identify the main issues, to break
down barriers between people so that they can face the questions
together, and to give them the hope and encouragement that will
inspire them to expect something to happen.

This 'secular' style of theology, which does not impose traditional Christian categories, but helps people to develop their
own thinking in their own terms, is essential to this kind of
exploration.

Of course what has been described is only a beginning. As the
search for meaning progresses, some people, but only some, will
see that there is more meaning in faith than they had supposed
and want to follow this up in some special way. For instance, a
group of managers, who had been working through some of the
questions they met in industry divided into two separate groups
so that some members could look more specifically at the meaning
of Christian faith. This group looked at the Christian understanding of God and of sin, and because they had been thinking
about their own experience in industry they were able to see that
sin is not only an individual but a corporate matter – an insight
seldom found in church congregations.

This last observation points to another frontier that should be
used creatively – that which exists between people inside the
churches and those outside who share a common concern to explore the meaning of faith. I am constantly struck by the way in
which the theological insights of people, who are for the most
part outside the church, can bring a fresh outlook to the theo-

logical thinking of church members. This style of approach to
theology is new to lay people and to clergy. This means that
clergy must be present in the areas where the issues arise, so that
they can work with lay people and learn together how faith and
life are related.

6. So far we have been discussing how issues are identified
and developed at the local level of concreteness – what may be
called the 'mini-scale'. The questions we have discussed are those
of people in a particular locality or factory. But if we think
through these issues we come up against much bigger issues which
cannot be dealt with on this mini-scale. For instance, local concern
with participation in planning cannot deal with the much larger
question of how the democratic institutions of our society are to
be enlivened so that the individual can play a responsible part.
The question of satisfaction in work cannot be answered simply
by discussion in one firm – or even one region or nation. We need
to keep on asking more questions – 'What are the causes of dissatisfaction? How can things be changed? What else is there
that might give satisfaction in life?' And these questions must be
tackled at a number of different levels at the same time. The
church must have the kind of organization that can relate what
is happening at the mini-level in order to deal with the same
questions at the maxi-level.

There are so many areas where the church ought to be contributing to thinking on the maxi-level. A fundamental critique
of the nature of industrial society, that is informed by real
understanding of what is happening in different industries and
in different regions, is needed. There is a vast vacuum in political
thinking, and those engaged in this field desperately need help
to create a new vision of the future and to free them from the
restraints of the past.

Economic growth as a goal has partially been discredited, but
the alternatives need spelling out. Only a few Christians are concerned enough to keep the needs of poor nations to the fore –
and so on.

Each individual can only see a little bit of what is happening.
Groups and institutions focus on their own interests. Different
people are trying to tackle different problems. Any coherence
there might have been has been broken up. But the fact is that
all these questions belong together, and are part of the whole
situation, so that no response can be adequate that does not
reckon with the whole situation. Industry needs to break out of
its own structures, ordinary people want to break into the decision-

making process of politics and planning; education wants to enter into dialogue with industry and so on. The church is meant to be a reconciling body. Its members must have the courage to think big, and to see how the different questions at their different levels of concreteness react upon each other. It is only as we are prepared to do this that the church can stand for the wholeness of human life in the present scene of change and fragmentation. To stand for wholeness is the church's distinctive function, but it is failing to do this because it is both theologically and organizationally unprepared. This book aims to spell out the theological needs of the task and it is from these that the organizational needs must be deduced.

7. No one should go away with the idea that these things can be done without conflict. If the church really gets involved in the issues of life it will get involved in conflict. It is a debilitating misunderstanding to see conflict as un-Christian. If we understood the total commitment of God to involvement in human life that the incarnation implies or if we understood crucifixion as the way to newness of life, we would see conflict in a much more positive way. The church should not be afraid to bring out the differences between people. The Kingdom of God – the *pleroma* – shalom – can only come when differences have been brought out and worked through. If we do not do that we must remain in a state of arrested development. Conflict, suffering and newness of life always must go together in the redemptive process. If we stick our necks out we must be prepared for conflict – but it is the only way to fullness of life. To take one example – a manager in a firm decided, against his directors' advice to involve the workers in decisions at the works for which he was responsible. He had been given the difficult job of running down a complete plant, including dealing with the redundancies that would be involved. He determined that, in the course of doing the job he had been given, he would make sure that each man had the opportunity to make a personal decision about his future. In order to do this he went far beyond what is usually understood by 'participation', sharing all information including financial statements with the men. The job was completed and it was recognized by everyone, including the directors, as a remarkably successful operation. For the manager concerned, however, there were other consequences. These were that, having completed this job he did not receive the promotion that had seemed to most people to be a matter of course, and was not offered any other job in the company. This is the risk that individuals take by

getting involved and this is the kind of risk that the church takes by its involvement – that is it must be ready to lose its life if it is to gain new life.

In this chapter I have pointed out the directions in which the church must go if it is to be in touch with the issues of life. If it does this it opens itself up to conflict and loss, but this is the only way it can keep life moving. Naturally we are fearful, but faith can overcome our fears so that we go forward with hope in the possibilities of new life:

'Men of little faith, why then do you fear or repudiate the progress of the world? Why foolishly multiply your warnings and your prohibitions? "Don't venture ... Don't try ... everything is known: the earth is empty and old: there is nothing more to be discovered."

'We must try everything for Christ; we must hope everything for Christ.... That, on the contrary, is the true Christian attitude....

'Jerusalem lift up your head. Look at the immense crowds of those who build and those who seek. All over the world, men are toiling – in laboratories, in studios, in deserts, in factories in the vast social crucible. The ferment that is taking place by their instrumentality in art and science and thought is happening for your sake. Open then, your arms and your heart, like Christ your Lord, and welcome the waters, the flood and the sap of humanity. Accept it, this sap – for, without its baptism, you will wither, without desire, like a flower out of water; and tend it, since, without your sun, it will disperse itself wildly in sterile shoots.'[4]

NOTES

1. Pierre Teilhard de Chardin, *Le Milieu Divin*, Collins 1960, p. 151.
2. Hendrik Kraemer, *A Theology of the Laity*, Lutterworth 1958, p. 176.
3. W. H. Wright, from an unpublished paper 1974.
4. Teilhard de Chardin, op. cit., p. 154.

IX

THE REVOLUTION OF THE LAITY

One thing should be clear by now and that is that what is needed is nothing less than a revolution of the laity. As things are, lay people are either lost in the world or trapped in the church. They must be freed and equipped to fulfil their ministry in the world. This chapter is about how this revolution can be helped by a two-pronged strategy that works from both outside and inside the church.

I shall start by discussing the kind of strategy that is needed outside the church. It is God's revolution not ours and it is going on in all sorts of ways and in all sorts of places. We cannot help unless we are aware of what is already happening, and most of this is happening outside not inside the church.

First of all I must give some examples of revolutionary change that is already under way, and from that point I shall suggest what the church's role may be in relation to them. The characteristic form of our society with its large organizations has led many people to try to discover ways in which there can be fuller participation in large institutions. A lot of experiment has been going on in industry, and in this region ICI has been a pace-setter. The firm has realized that technological change demands greater flexibility in the organization and its workers, and has therefore undertaken a sustained programme of behavioural change, so that they now employ some of the most experienced behavioural scientists and organization development men in the country. In the various processes they use, the unstructured situation is central. This has had the effect of liberating people from their constraints and opening them up to newness and changes in behaviour. As far as the firm is concerned the effect has been a development in shared responsibility and new styles of management. For the members it has often meant tension and strain for it is never easy to change, but most of those who have been involved are enthusiastic about their experiences, and what they say about it all has many of the signs of evangelical revival. Working in this way has opened up a new dimension of life and stimulated new questions about meaning, which they see are relevant not only to their work but to other aspects of life. They are more than ready to share this search for meaning with others in the community and to contribute some of the skills that are needed in that search. Here is one area where revolution is already happening.

The need for greater participation is also an issue in the political field. The most significant movement here is in the small groups that are trying to make their views heard on specific issues. These issues may concern the routing of a new road or housing priorities, or they may relate to world poverty or race relations. Most of the groups include people of widely different political views, and some of these, especially the younger ones, are putting fundamental questions against society as it now is – with its emphasis on goals of growth and consumption. So far, Christian involvement is hesitant, in spite of the fact that some of these groups were actually started by the church. We have already noted that the participation of Christians in anything political is minimal, and that they show a marked preference for the caring organizations like Samaritans and Meals on Wheels.[1] Yet this is surely one of the areas where new things are happening and questions about meaning are most urgent.

In the North East region questions about employment and unemployment are uppermost in many people's minds. There is a sense of impotence and the feeling that decisions about the economy are made at a distance without any real understanding of their effects on the region. A number of issues are involved – from the immediate question of new jobs to a concern about growth as a proper goal for society. Many people are working on these questions but the matter is too big to be tackled in a piece-meal way and nothing radically new is emerging.

This is one of the issues where the church has got involved, and a description of some action taken by the church can throw light on the kind of strategy it should employ when working with groups outside itself. In view of a general concern about rising unemployment in the region, the Teesside Council of Churches with the Teesside Industrial Mission suggested that a conference should take place that would involve a representative group of Teessiders including church representatives, with some economists from London. The purpose would be to try to under-

stand the situation from the point of view of the London economists as well as from the experiences of people in Teesside who
were affected by their policies. Although the emphasis would be
on action, this would not simply be concerned with how more
jobs could be brought to the region, but with questions of how
economic and technological issues affect the quality of life on
Teesside. A planning group that included managers, trade
unionists and economists as well as church representatives was
set up to prepare the consultation and in March 1973 about
thirty people met in Teesside for two days.

From the mixed membership of the consultation it follows that
there was considerable disagreement. A number of people considered that the lack of entrepreneural abilities in the area was
a main defect that must be attributed to the domination of a
few large firms. An ambitious plan was directed towards fostering
entrepreneural initiatives. But the trade unionists declared that
they would not be party to this kind of development of the
capitalistic system, and that solutions for them lay in pressing
for more jobs of a traditional kind in the area. When it was
pointed out that a new situation demands new solutions and
new initiatives they said that their views were based on a realistic
reading of the present situation while others were looking too
far into the future. Progress can only take place when both points
of view are taken into account in order to move on to something
new.

Behind these disagreements lie fundamental questions: What
should be the goals of our society – growth – no growth or limited
growth? How does the goal of growth relate to the quality of life
and to the true purpose of human life? What can an individual
or any group of people do in the face of economic forces? One
member remarked that fatalism is the prevailing mood in most
discussions of this kind.

These are only some of the questions that were raised, but
this is enough to show that these are questions about the meaning
of life and that therefore questions about the meaning of faith
are also involved.

I was a member of this consultation and I could see that there
was a job here for a theologian. People were aware of a whole
range of issues but were not at all clear what the essential questions
were or what direction to take. Each person's viewpoint had been
shaped by the particular interests of his own group and his
responses were within patterns formed by past history. Each had
an essential bit of experience to share, but none could see the

whole picture. All needed to be freed from their past, to become more appreciative of other experiences and other points of view and to be more open to a different future. All wanted to appear as practical people but unless they were confronted with the need for change both in themselves and in their situation they would only continue to repeat the same patterns that had led to the present unsatisfactory state of affairs.

These are points to which every Christian should have something to contribute from his own understanding of life and of faith. The problem lies in knowing what is the appropriate way to do this in this kind of setting.

It clearly does not help to introduce religion as something to be imposed on the situation as if Christianity had its own ready made answer, nor does it help to start using religious language. The starting point must be the conviction that no understanding of or response to the situation can be adequate unless we reckon with the fact of God in the situation. This does not mean talking about God but talking about the situation from the point of view of faith in God.

This is so obvious that it should not need stating – for in fact whatever anyone says he speaks out of his own faith or philosophy of life. The problem with Christians is that they have separated faith and life so that they operate on two separate philosophies, one for their home and church and another for business and public life. The revolution of the laity must involve bringing faith to bear on every part of life.

At this particular consultation there was some confusion about the place of Christian faith and the role of the church. This happened because the Christians who had initiated the consultation were not in agreement themselves. There was an odd alliance between representatives of Mission 'A', who considered that Christianity had nothing to do with questions about society, and representatives of Mission 'B' who considered that all that was required of them was simply to be involved. They thought they had done enough by getting the consultation set up, and saw no place for theology in the preparation, the follow up or the consultation itself.

Both 'A' and 'B' had completely misunderstood the nature of theology and its place in this consultation. Yet this should have been obvious for everyone in the group was concerned to find meaning and to see the situation whole. Questions were being put against the conventional ways of understanding life and responding to it. Fundamental issues were being raised about what men and women are for, what the possibilities of life are, and what resources are available for living. This is what Christianity is about and it is around these questions that theology must be done.

To 'do theology' is to try to understand a particular situation in the light of Christian faith. Simply to look at things in this way enables one to see the demands and possibilities of the situation in a distinctive way. 'Doing theology' is a joint effort, it means learning from each other, distinguishing differences, uncovering some of their causes and a host of other things. All this can be done as part and parcel of the whole debate, and there is no need to introduce some special religious language, or separate time when we 'do theology' as if we were not doing it all the time.

Of course this is only a start, and was in fact all that was possible at this kind of consultation. But there is a way of sparking off new ideas that can be followed up later – and it is important to do just that. This is important for two reasons, first of all for the people at the consultation – some of whom may be set on to new lines of exploration, and secondly for the church itself.

On this occasion, I was particularly anxious to feed some of the questions that were thrown up at this consultation back to the church, for I believe the church must make a more critical theological assessment of the goals of our industrial society on a maxi-scale in the light of information it receives from the local level.

But as I have shown, we failed to 'do theology' in the way I had hoped. The confusion among the church members inevitably aroused anxieties among the non-church members, whose past experience made them fear that religion was going to 'be dragged in' and would confuse the practical aims of the consultation.

I mention this failure in order to show that both Mission 'A' and Mission 'B' in their extreme forms are failing to meet the needs of a revolution of the laity. What we must do is to find ways of doing theology in which the questions of life and the insights of the gospel come together.

Some hopeful things are happening in small ways. I am working with a group consisting mainly of men from industry, who came together because their contact with an industrial chaplain made them aware that Christianity might have some relevance to the questions they met in their working lives. We have had to develop a particular style of theology for they were not prepared to be lectured at but wanted a theologian to help them work through their own questions. Some members of the group started almost from scratch in their exploration of Christian faith, but others like Ernie, have had to escape from the church in order to feel free to explore the questions that really concern them. Groups of this kind are a natural outcome of the work of 'sector' ministries and make it abundantly clear that the debate about the meaning of faith must be more than a private debate within the church.

The common factor in this kind of group is serious concern about issues of daily life and theology is integral to everything else that is discussed. It is a joint enterprise in which the skills, experience and insights of all are needed. It is out of the experience of the members that some elements of Christian faith come to life. Love, justice and truth are no longer abstract themes but take on substance as they are seen in relation to concrete situations and particular actions: sin is recognized as something that gets into groups and institutions as well as into individuals; and Christianity is seen to be relevant to the grey areas of life where all choices are less than perfect. While these themes emerge in an exciting way, other essential aspects of Christian faith are never mentioned. This is why I am convinced that groups like this need the help of a theologian who can relate the group's thinking to the larger context of Christian theology and introduce ideas that are new to the members.

I have described one consultation and the work of one group of lay people but this is only scratching the surface, and more needs to be done if a revolution of the laity is to take place.

My purpose in setting this out is to argue that work with lay people outside the churches must become a recognized part of the church's strategy, and that the church should spend as much time with groups outside the church as it does with groups inside the church. At present very few people see how urgent this is and the whole way the church is organized makes it impossible. Nothing less than revolution is needed here.

What is needed is something on the scale of the lay academies in Germany. These only came into existence because the church was forced by World War II to realize the urgent need for it to make some contribution to the questions of a technological society.

The chief characteristics of the Academy Movement are: to start with the questions of life, to bring together cross-sections of those concerned with a particular issue (whether they are Christian or not is immaterial); to treat those who come as contributors not pupils; and to carry through the meetings in a secular style, in which the Christian message is an integral part of the issues discussed, and the gospel is discussed as frankly as anything else. The idea of the academy should not be connected with the country mansions and castles which house the German academies, but should be seen as the building up of a network of skills and services for use in all sorts of different situations. William Temple College, which now has no building of its own, is the best example of the attempt to develop this kind of network in this country. This is a living image of the kind of way in which the church should be working.

When lay development starts from life instead of from the church, a number of problems are by-passed. The most obvious is that the frontier between the church and the world is crossed by concentration on questions that are common to both sides. Secondly, denominational barriers become irrelevant. But even more fundamental is the fact that people can be brought together from a broad enough front to deal with questions that could not be tackled by any one congregation or even several congregations working together.

I have already mentioned that the questions raised by the secular groups that we noticed in chapter V – the economy, scientific and technical change, and so on – must be dealt with on a broad front, while the congregation who produced questions about pornography and abortion, need to see their questions in a bigger context.

It has been said[2] that there are six main areas of lay responsibility for the modern Christian:

1. His church duties.
2. His family and sexual personal relationships.
3. His neighbourhood responsibilities.
4. His participation in industrial, commercial and economic life.
5. His leisure time.
6. His participation in public life and politics.

'It could be argued that many churches (particularly the more go-ahead suburban ones both in Britain and in the United States) do quite a reasonable job on Nos. 1 to 3 above,' though there are others which restrict themselves entirely to instruction in no. 1. It is possible for nos. 1 to 3 to be dealt with by the local congregation, though there would be obvious benefit if churches and denominations co-operated within a locality. When it comes to nos. 4 to 6, however, we have to admit that a very large number of Christian laity are almost hopelessly illiterate. These topics cannot be adequately dealt with from within the local congregation. They need the co-operation of people from a wider area than that covered by a single parish. They need the help of people with specific experience and skills from outside the church, and they need the back-up of specialist services within the church itself such as that which can be brought by the minister who has been set aside to spend his whole time in the field of industry, politics, leisure and so on. If this is taken seriously it requires completely new planning for laity development within the church – what this entails in practice will be expanded in the next chapter.

The point that must be made now is that the six areas of lay responsibility need to be held together by a common understanding of the way theology must be done as a part of the whole exploration.

What is required is a style of doing theology that starts from life and that can involve Christians and non-Christians together: it presupposes a number of lay people who feel that the way they have been taught to think about their faith has been restricting and who now want to explore fundamental questions without restriction.

The demands of doing theology in this way are immense and new ways of equipping clergy and lay people for this new situation are urgently needed and they must be on the scale that I have indicated. Many people will say it is impossible for the church in this country to do anything of the kind, and they will point to a shortage of money and manpower. I shall show, however, in the next chapter that the resources we have could be more effectively used if a strategy of this kind was adopted. It is not money and men we are short of, so much as understanding of what the job is.

Now, I want to leave the question of work with people outside the church and look at what must be done with people inside the church.

I have insisted on the need for a revolution of the laity to be encouraged from outside the church, and I shall insist with equal urgency for that revolution also to be encouraged from inside the church.

'Revolution' hardly seems the right word for the painfully slow process of change at St Cuthbert's Church. This is a parish with a population of 10,000 people housed partly in private and partly in council housing. The present vicar, whose first incumbency it is, has been there for about eight years. He admits that for the first three years he wondered what he was meant to be doing and how long he could stand it. A few lay people had everything in their hands and no one else had a look-in. Resistance to change was concentrated on things like the control of finance and the use of the church hall, which was reserved almost exclusively for the needs of the drama group. This came to an end with the inevitable confrontation, which was painful and nerve-racking for the vicar who risked losing many of the congregation and the financial viability of the church. All this is such a familiar story that it is hardly worth mentioning, but it stresses the cost of change in a congregation and that the brunt of this falls on the vicar and his wife.

The positive aims of the task were not at first apparent – even now they are not clear because Christian life is always a response to the movement of God's Spirit in a changing situation. But the general outline has crystallized into the task of promoting the formation of a Christian community, the marks of which shall be eucharistic – that is that it shall worship God; accepting – that is, it shall be a community in which those who are unacceptable find grace by being accepted; and newness of life. This task has two aspects – the journey outwards towards other people and into action in life in the world, and the journey inwards towards self-awareness and a knowledge of God. Both journeys are interrelated and it is impossible to make progress in one without progressing in the other. The vicar thinks that people are scared by both journeys, but that a number of people are in fact embarking on the journey outwards – and that the church has a special responsibility for the journey inwards. It may even be that for some the journey outwards is being used as an escape from looking inwards at themselves. His own efforts are therefore concentrated on helping people with the journey inwards.

He sees this as helping people to become fully themselves – real people in relation with other people. A number of activities are contributing to the process. These include congregational week-ends with un-structured programmes, helped on two occasions by one of the behavioural scientists who has recently left ICI, and on another occasion by the Diocesan Adviser for Lay Training; an open house at the vicarage on Sundays twice each month, from about 11-5 for anyone to come and talk or 'do their own thing'. In addition, a group of ten people, including the vicar and curate and their wives, have committed themselves to what they call a 'gifts' course in which they are acting as 'guinea-pigs' for the rest of the congregation. This course has been held each Sunday evening for the last eighteen weeks and has consisted of exploration into silence and prayer, discovery of their own gifts and talents and recognition of those of others. The course is based on work done in a Washington parish, USA, the books on prayer by Anthony Bloom and the experience of the members themselves. Behind this lies extensive exploration made by the vicar in order to discover resources for renewal within church tradition and practice. A further activity that is being discussed during the informal meetings at the vicarage is the setting up of house groups, and the need to help those lay people who are showing signs of ability to lead them.

In this process of change there have been some major discoveries. I have already pointed out the slowness of the process and the time and energy that must be put into it by both clergy and laity. This suggests a danger of the church becoming overconcerned with its own internal life to the exclusion of all else. This is a real danger. This is why it is essential for the church to have a two-pronged strategy. Work must be going on in the world as well as in the congregation because there is an urgency that means we cannot afford to wait. At the same time we should admit how difficult it is for any of us to change – and that it may only be possible to make the kind of changes that are needed in our own behaviour if we are supported by an accepting community. It is out of the security of real acceptance by a small group that love can become an over-riding motivation in all situations.

Somehow or other, people have been taught in the church to undervalue themselves (often this includes a devaluation of all that is physical) – yet the gospel affirms the unique value of each individual in his wholeness, his unique gifts and his personal call from God. It is only as people discover that they matter as individuals that they can discover what it means to be the church and to be a sign to the world of the true nature of human community.

People may have learnt something about resurrection, salvation, grace, repentance and forgiveness – though even this is often in doubt – but if they do not experience these things in their relationships with others they will not understand what these mean and 'the penny will never drop'.

The old styles of leadership must change, but there must still be leadership. This must be given by all sorts of people in different ways and in different situations, but responsibility for giving direction and purpose to the overall enterprise remains that of the vicar. This is a demanding, personal, spiritual and theological task and the person who does it must himself have counsel and support. In view of the fact of this leadership it is unrealistic to talk about a revolution of the laity unless steps are taken to help the clergy come to terms with changes in their role at the same time. We will return to this point later, and I shall also return to the question of the outside resources that are needed to help forward the revolution at the parish level. But first I want to put this single example of revolution within one congregation in a bigger context.

Everyone is aware that there is a revolution going on in the Roman Catholic Church, but we are less familiar with what impact this is making on the local congregation. One priest summed up the change by saying that people were coming to see that they were not involved in a system of ideas, but in a living relationship with a person. The main instrument of change is the liturgy and the changes taking place in it. Everything is geared towards making clear that the meaning of faith is a relationship with Christ and that the inescapable corollary of commitment to Christ is commitment to the love and service of all men.

So challenging are the changes that some people leave their parish church in the attempt to find a church that is not changing – with of course parallel movement in the other direction. The main job to be done is to help people get rid of their 'dead theology'. This requires opportunity for discussion and a chance to question authority and to take responsibility upon oneself. The practical changes towards this are the participation of the laity in the liturgy, parish councils and family groups.

There is no obligation on a parish to set up a parish council, so that where a parish priest does do this it means he genuinely wants to de-clericalize the church and to involve lay people in policy issues. The family groups are the main form of adult development, and, even where there are no parish councils, considerable lay leadership is developing as people meet in each other's homes to discuss points of Christian faith in relation to life.

A further aspect of renewal in the Roman Catholic Church is the explicit concern with social justice. The incentive for this comes at the parish level from people gaining a clearer understanding of what is involved in their commitment to Christ in the mass, at another level the Commission for International Justice and Peace gives further encouragement as it makes the experience of Roman Catholics in other parts of the world available to Christians in this country.

Each denomination has its own diocesan or district system

of support for what is happening on the local level. In 1966 the Darlington Methodist District Synod set up a working party to explore ways in which congregations could be helped to make the changes necessary to the fulfilment of their missionary task. As a result an experimental consultancy service was set up headed by two ministers and a sociologist, with a good deal of help from organization development men who were working on ways of facilitating change in industry. The consultants offered to work for about six months with any congregation who accepted their offer. During this time they would help the congregation study its relationship with its environment, and determine its priorities. Initially this involved three meetings with those whom the church decided were its leaders – the people included in this group varied with each congregation. When the pilot scheme had been properly tested the intention was to involve a leadership group from all the congregations in a continuing training scheme in order to develop a pool of consultants.

A number of discoveries were made during this exploration. First of all it was found that the congregations did not know what the problems of their communities were. This was particularly evident in some of the mining villages which had been scheduled as category 'D' – which meant that no further development could take place in them, and that as living communities they faced slow extinction. Congregations actually in category 'D' villages did not even mention this as a matter of concern or see that it raised real problems. They seemed unable to discuss anything political or conflictive and when it came to deciding on some project that would involve them in the community, they invariably chose a service project like work with old people. Another blind spot was their relation to other denominations, and any practical move to work with the Anglicans or any other congregation in the area was avoided. It is important to note that it was the fact that there were outside resources that helped these blind spots to be opened up.

There were some outstanding successes and one of these has resulted in the establishment of an ecumenical parish in the town of Guisborough.

In spite of this, however, the project has temporarily come to a halt. Various reasons may be given for this – some of the people involved moved away from the district, the sheer effort needed to keep the thing moving proved too much for the key people in the enterprise; but perhaps the main reason was resistance from the local ministers which meant that the offer of help was simply not taken up. This points to what should be obvious that any revolution of the laity will be blocked unless there is at the same time a revolution of the clergy.

Release from bondage and from all that constrains and inhibits free growth is the message of the gospel. In a number of ways lay people do not feel free to open up and expand into the life that is freely offered to us in Christ. The revolution of the laity is about realizing that freedom. Christ's resurrection is the climax of the struggle for freedom and for life that is the main theme of the Bible, and the bursting of the tomb points to the final release of all creation. Today 'the world which needs to be raised from the dead, waits for the revelation of the "glorious liberty of the children of God" '.[3]

I have shown that the church must have a two-fold strategy for this revolution, and I want to finish this chapter by pointing to some of the specific things that must be done:

1. Misconceptions about the needs of the laity must be removed. There are conflicting views about what lay people need. The first considers that the need is for information that must be passed on to lay people – by the clergy. This has been called an education for 'domestication',[4] it does not train for liberty or encourage people to bring forward any critical questions but only for obedience and the repetition of what others say. But the second view recognizes that freedom means saying one's own words, and the revolution of the laity must help people to break out from a passive attitude of unquestioning acceptance in order to discover and speak their own word. This is a matter of transformation rather than information.

2. This means that the whole style of what is done must be participative. Participation must take place at all stages and not least in the actual planning of any project. I pointed out that the programme of the employment consultation in Teesside was planned by a representative group. The same group was asked if they wished to mount a conference on the impact of oil and steel developments in the area, but decided against it. People have to decide what they feel will help and not simply carry out someone else's plans.

3. A participative style of work replaces a teacher/pupil relationship with a relationship of mutual give and take in which everyone is both teacher and learner.

4. This means a radical change in the clergy/lay relationship. For both clergy and laity this is one of the hardest changes to make. Much of the church's life assumes that the clergyman is

the shepherd of a 'flock' whose job it is to follow him, and some people among both clergy and laity like it this way. Any change causes considerable confusion and insecurity. Nor will change happen unless there is some re-training of clergy preferably with lay people.

5. The revolution of the laity will not happen as the result of a simple strategy, but a lot of things must happen at the same time. I have shown that there must be a two-pronged strategy of work both outside the church and inside. This requires a diversity of ministries so that clergy are working in all the main areas of life with the neighbourhood church as only one among others. There must also be work on the different levels – local, regional, national and international.

There is a strong pull in the church towards uniformity of ministry and anxieties are always being expressed about the 'irregularity' of newer forms of ministry, but a diversity of ministry is essential in a diversified society.

6. To have a diversity of operation and ministry should not mean that everyone goes their own way regardless of anyone else. One of the things we are trying to get away from is the fragmentation of our efforts and if this is to be avoided there must be effective management within the church. The word 'management' raises for many people all the wrong ideas – so I must insist that I am not talking about some sort of dictatorship. It is unfortunate that the church only seems to have two models of management, that of the 'Prince Bishop' who has absolute authority and a *'laissez faire'* model in which anything goes. Yet industry is learning so much about new participative styles of management, and there are many church members who are also managers and who have considerable experience which they could share. We must replace a hierarchical model of the church with an organic model within which all sorts of networks of communication and co-operation can be developed. This means that instead of the present atmosphere of distrust and insecurity, we must cultivate an atmosphere of communication, trust and mutual accountability.

This will change the relationship between different departments and between different denominations. I am not proposing premature amalgamations for this can simply mean that the church draws in on itself rather than extending out into the world.

7. Cross-fertilization between people involved in different aspects of the revolution must take place in all sorts of ways. For

instance, a man whose only connection with the church is his membership of an open discussion group on questions of daily life, joined in a meeting of a local council of churches who were working out a statement of faith for evangelistic use. He brought their discussions down to earth by pointing out that words like 'redemption' and 'sin' had little content for anyone outside their own group. Another member of the same open discussion group, who is also an industrial training officer, led a series of trainings on group discussion with some clergy. A network of give and take develops when people begin to appreciate their own needs and the particular skills of people who are not in their own immediate circle.

Cross-fertilization must also occur between the different levels – local, regional, national and international. This should not simply be a matter of people at the centre receiving information from people at the local level and passing instructions down to them, but should be a matter of mutual learning. One of the aims of the Teesside employment consultation was that there should be mutual learning between economists from London and the Teesside people who were affected by their policies. Each had something to learn from the other.

8. For any change to take place there must be some sort of 'change agents'. The consultancy service of the Methodist Church in the Darlington district is an example of this, and so is my own theological consultancy. Through the work of this kind of consultancy the problems and possibilities of change can be identified and processed for the benefit of the whole church.

9. Theology in this kind of revolution, takes on a new complexion. It can no longer be seen as communicating a system of ideas, but as drawing out the meaning of life. This means that it cannot simply be part of the 'syllabus', to be introduced at some appropriate point, but must be integral to the whole process. It must help people grasp the vision and purpose of the whole enterprise: it must identify the questions that must be tackled at each stage: it must provide information from a wide range of sources including the varied traditions of the whole church: it must discover potential resources and skills and help in their development. It is theology and new ways of doing theology that constitutes and carries forward the revolution of the laity. It is this kind of revolution that I am involved in with others in the North East.

One of the most urgent tasks that arises from this new understanding of the place of theology is the need to create a systematic

plan for the development and use of all *resources*. This is so
central to the revolution that we must now turn our attention
to it.

NOTES

1. B. Cooper, J. Rimmer & M. Sweeting, *Structuring the Church for Mission*, Belton Books 1969, a survey of the participation of church members in non-church voluntary organizations in Teesside.
2. Mark Gibbs & T. Ralph Morton, *God's Lively People*, Collins 1971, p. 106.
3. Rom. 8.21, quoted in E. Käsemann, *Jesus Means Freedom*, SCM Press 1969, p. 155.
4. Paulo Freire, *Pedagogy of the Oppressed*, Penguin Books 1972.

X

DEVELOPING THE RESOURCES

The main question that the church must face is 'How can we do theology so that men and women can discover resources and hopes, corrections and encouragements in all that they have to face?' The job is so immense that it is not surprising that some people point to the shortage of manpower and money in the church – and say that it is impossible. In this chapter I want to show that potentially there are a lot of resources and that what is needed is a systematic plan for their development and use.

Behind the church's failure to work out a plan and strategy for the development of the necessary resources is the failure to understand what it means for theology to be done in and for an industrial society.

Technology and industry determine the characteristics of our society. It is industry that has led to the concentration of the population in large cities and conurbations. It is technology that has made the whole world interdependent, so that the Arab sheikhs can change the lives of people throughout the world. It is changes in technology that lead to the continual movement of people from one area to another – deciding that the mining villages of West Durham shall die while the population of South East England multiplies. Technology has created communities that, instead of being derived from the place of residence, are derived from the place people have in relation to the great institutions of society – education, industry, local government, etc. Whether we like it or not, it still remains true that technology and industry create the context within which we must search for meaning in life.

But the church is not geared to working with people in these newer forms of community for it still clings to the old static model of society and to the ideal of the small self-contained community based on the place of residence. Within this pattern it retains

Type of Course	Sponsors	Membership		Resources being used
I Work with Lay People				
(*a*) Outside the Church				*The experience of the members*
Monthly meeting of men from industry studying faith in relation to questions of life	Industrial mission and Durham Extra-Mural Department	People from industry		
Three-day conferences for men and women from industry to explore questions of work and faith	Industrial missions	People from industry	T H	Industrialists, trade unionists, economists, sociologists
Behavioural science courses for the exploration of personal and inter-personal behaviour	Durham University Business School, Newcastle Polytechnic, Industrial firms, private consultancies	The general public, industrial firms	E O	Behavioural scientists
Special issues, 'frontier' groups and consultations:			L O	
Employment consultation	Teesside Council of Churches, Teesside Industrial Mission	Economists, church representatives, cross-section of Teesside people	G	Economists
The place of art and leisure in life	Arts and recreation chaplain	Artists, teachers, local government officials and councillors	Y	Artists, teachers, local government officials and councillors

		Members	The experience of the members
Medical/ethical issues	Hospital chaplain	Doctors, hospital and health service staff, public	Doctors, psychologists
Poverty action group, race relations, drugs	Community action groups	General public, minority groups, police, social services	Economists, people from minority groups, police, social workers
Police and community	Social responsibility officer	Police and representatives of community and caring professions, general public	
Community development	Local authority and community and church bodies		Experienced community development workers
(b) Inside the Church			
Congregational development 'the journey inward'	Local church (C of E)	Members of the congregation	Behavioural scientists
Congregational development 'the journey outward'	Methodist district synod (Darlington)	Leaders within each local church	Sociologists, organization and development men from industry
Congregational development, spiritual re-orientation	Diocese of Hexham and Newcastle Pastoral Centre (RC)	Members of congregations	
II Clergy and Laity			
Role of the church in urban industrial society	Teesside Industrial Mission, Teesside Council of Churches, Durham Extra-Mural Department	Clergy and lay people from the same congregations in Teesside	Sociologists, industrialists, trade unionists, local government officials, politicians, economists,

T
H
E
O
L
O
G
Y

Type of Course	Sponsors	Membership		Resources being used
	Durham Diocese, Durham Extra-Mural Department, Sunderland Council of Churches	do. in Sunderland	T	clergy and lay people with special experience of work in urban areas
Frontier issues: Unemployment	Teesside Industrial Mission	Clergy and lay people in Teesside	H	Economists, industrialists, unemployed, social workers and members of Departments of Employment and of Social Security.
Energy crisis	Newcastle Diocesan Synod	Synod members of Newcastle Diocese	E	Fuel experts, trade unionists
World religions – the search for meaning	Darlington College of Education, Newcastle Polytechnic	Clergy and social workers of any denomination	O	
Philosophical – the search for meaning	Teesside Polytechnic	Teachers, clergy, general public	L	Philosophers, political philosophers, behavioural scientists, sociologists
III Work with Clergy				
Practical: team ministry etc.	Further training, Durham Diocese	Clergy – team members	O	Organization and development men from industry
Two-day introduction to ministry in industrial society	Industrial missions	Clergy of all denominations in the region	G	Industrialists, trade unionists, industrial chaplains
Biblical and doctrinal	Further training, Durham Diocese	Open to all clergy in Durham Diocese	Y	

its belief that a resident minister can serve the needs of people in a personal way within each specific geographical area.

I have shown that in spite of the inappropriateness of its basic model, the church is trying to respond to the new needs of industrial society. It has appointed some industrial chaplains and social responsibility officers, it has created team ministries and undertaken new forms of ecumenical work, but because it is totally committed to its present understanding of community and patterns of working, it insists on pulling everything back to fit the old model.

This prevents the church from facing the real needs of society and for this reason nothing less than a revolution is needed. This revolution must involve a complete change in the church's understanding of how God is at work in the world – that is a change in theology; it must involve a change in the church's centre of interest and activity from the church to the world, and a change of emphasis from the clergy to the laity as the initiators of mission.

The crux of the matter lies in recognizing that the need is to help men and women to live hopefully and creatively with the questions which their life puts to their humanity.

The basis of the church's response to this need is the belief that God in Jesus has done and is doing something for us and that what he is doing can be discovered as part of our living and hoping.

In this way the question about resources becomes a question about how resources can be found that will enable theology to be done in the world.

In spite of the apparent difficulties, I believe that a survey of any area will show immense resources. My own experience in the North East has convinced me of this and I do not believe that in this respect the North East is different from any other area.

I have already mentioned a number of ways in which the church is helping people in the search for meaning in this region and some of the varied resources that are being used to do this. When these are drawn together, the list becomes impressive. Consider for instance the examples I have drawn together in the table on pages 118-120.

These are all things that are actually happening. They are only examples from a mass of other things that are also going on. For instance, I have left out everything to do with young people. Most of what I have mentioned has been started by the church but much more important things are being done by other organizations. Even within these limits the list represents a random selection from many other activities, but this should be enough to make the points that need making.

The church is involved in one way or another in a lot of different activities in which a number of different resources are being used.

The table sets out exactly what these resources are. Starting at the left-hand column with the sponsors it is clear that the church does not have to set up all the courses itself, for there are other institutions which see it as part of their job to help people engage in the search for meaning. These institutions are in themselves resources for theology and they include Durham University Extra-Mural Department, Durham University Business School, polytechnics and colleges of education. All have some responsibility in the field of adult education and all are in a position to bring together a number of different disciplines that are essential to the search for meaning in today's world.

Membership of the courses, which is listed in the second column, may be open to the general public or limited to specific groups in society in order to help them find meaning in their own particular situations. Courses may involve people from outside or inside the churches or a mixture of both. Some courses involve a cross-section of people who have a concern with the same issue.

When it comes to actually 'doing theology', the chief resources that are needed are those that are most often overlooked, that is the skills and experience of course members themselves. This is why this resource is italicized at the top of the last two columns. The main objective of any course should be to release, use and develop the abilities of its members. But too often there is a dependence on 'experts' brought in from outside. However experienced the members may be it is assumed that they come as 'learners' and that someone else must come as 'teacher'. This assumption must be replaced by the belief that everyone comes as both teacher and learner. On this view a course takes on a different shape and style. Members then work together to identify the questions that concern them, and pursue their own exploration of the issues using their joint resources as far as they possibly can. There is far more potential in people than we think and the resources of a group should be pushed as far as possible. It is only when these resources are exhausted that there is need to look round for outside help. By that time the members of the group will know exactly what kind of outside help is relevant.

The right-hand column lists some of the additional skills that may be brought into play when group members have stretched their own resources as far as possible. First there is need for the sociologist and behavioural scientist. For example, I have already referred to the fact that congregations are often unable to recognize the real questions that face their own communities. A sociologist can open up a completely new understanding of a situation by challenging the interpretations that are offered by a group. His skill is needed to evaluate the group's observations and to show how their own particular assumptions and prejudices have made them blind to some important factors in their situation. Another skill that is needed in any work with groups is that of the group worker or behavioural scientist.

Secondly there are times when the group does not have sufficient spread of experience among its own members to deal with the particular question with which they are concerned. Those who attended the conferences for people from industry, for instance, often only knew their own industry or even only one department in it. It was therefore helpful to invite someone with broader experience to come in. This is not always a matter of bringing in 'top' people for many church groups have been helped by an injection of experience from the disadvantaged and the unemployed.

Thirdly there is need for other specific disciplines – such as economics, political science and philosophy.

The word 'theology' runs down from the top to the bottom of the resources column, alongside every entry that is in it. This is meant to emphasize the fact that the key resource that is needed in all these courses and consultations is theology. For instance, in the first course on the list, people came together because they wanted to find the meaning of the questions they were facing in industry and saw the possibility of Christian faith being relevant. In the behavioural science courses people face the reality and the meaning of their own behaviour and that of others in group and inter-group relations. In dealing with special issues like employment and unemployment people examine the facts, and also explore the meaning of those facts in order to determine relevant action. In every case because theology is about meaning it is not only relevant but necessary to the exploration.

As with the other resources, the most important theological resources are those of the members themselves. It is the person who is actually in a situation who has unique clues to the meaning of that situation. There are, however, additional theological skills that are needed, and if they are not present in the group they must be found somewhere else. There is need to draw out the theological contributions of the members and to help them to articulate their faith. There is need for a sense of direction so that the group moves forward instead of retreating when things become difficult, and there are times when new insights must be offered from the whole range of Christian theology. This requires the best that academic theology can give, but because the data of life is also essential the professional theologian must himself remain a co-searcher for truth.

Though theology has been a real part of some of these courses there are others where it has not been a significant factor. I have for instance already mentioned the employment consultation on Teesside and described the difficulties that stopped theology from being a useful factor on that occasion. The seriousness of this gap must be recognized for without theology the activities referred to in the table easily becomes mere activism.

The table shows that there have been a whole lot of different responses to the new needs of an industrial society, and I have tried to show in this book how immense these needs are. *Ad hoc* responses to these needs are totally inadequate because the needs arise from changes in society that affect man's total understanding of life. This demands a total response from the church. It is all right for pioneering to be done, but the results need to be examined and their significance for the church as a whole taken into account. If important projects continue to grow in an *ad hoc* way it can only lead to confusion and waste of resources. My argument now is for a systematic development and use of all the potential resources and energies within some over-arching vision and strategy.

The table shows that at present things, 'like Topsy', are just growing. How much better all this would be if there were some planning behind it. As it is things have reached the point of buzzing confusion, and the scattered action has reached the stage of being self-defeating, when it is inevitable that there will be overlap, over extension and collapse.

In this kind of situation it is the most successful operations that are doomed to failure. The social responsibility officer for instance, who gains the confidence of elected members and officials of a local authority may find work opening up that he cannot possibly tackle by himself, but, because his work has no place in any long-term strategy of the church, he has to let the opportunities pass or drive himself to some sort of breakdown.

We have already seen that the Methodist consultancy service

had to suspend its operations because the pressure on those who were responsible for it became too great. This is a typical case of a lack of forward planning, so that at the very moment when new ground had been broken and things were ready to expand, the necessary resources were not available. If there is no plan everything depends on the individual; if he moves away or is taken ill, the project collapses with the corollary that at some future date the whole cycle will start all over again, without any lessons being learnt.

In addition the lack of planning leads to overlap, with the tensions and conflict this entails. However limited the initial responses may be, it is impossible to keep them in water-tight compartments – for before long people must become aware of the fact that the questions they are tackling raise the whole issue of the meaning of life and of faith. Even more damaging is the fact that where there is no plan, the most valuable resources are so over-extended that they are in danger of being totally destroyed. We have all met the loyal church layman who ends up by living at church. The same sort of thing can happen when the sociologist, behavioural scientist or a good discussion group leader is used in an *ad hoc* way.

An illustration of the complexity of the situation and the need for systematization may be given by describing one of the courses that needed a particularly wide spectrum of skills. This was a course on 'The Role of the Church in Urban/Industrial Society' held in Sunderland. I described in chapter VII how Sunderland was the subject of a commission, whose main recommendation was that the church should aim to work ecumenically as one team throughout the whole town. Sunderland is a town of some 200,000 people with 26 Anglican parishes, so the proposal represented a considerable challenge.

The course was planned as one contribution towards helping response to this challenge to wholeness. The programme gave an introduction to different aspects of Sunderland's life and provided opportunities for considering the meaning of ministry in this setting. A dozen clergy enrolled and a course of three separate weeks, non-residential, took place during 1972. This was followed by a week-end for lay people from the same churches and some joint meetings of clergy and laity.

All I want to do here is to list the actual resources that were used. Each week gave an introduction to a particular aspect of the life of the town. During the first week which was concerned with 'The Family and Community in Urban Society', the following outside resources were used; a sociology lecturer from Newcastle University, the Sunderland Director of Social Services, local government officials, local councillors and the Church's Social Responsibility Officer for Teesside. During the second week, which was concerned with 'The Nature of Industrial Society', the following people helped: lecturers in politics and in industrial relations from Sunderland Polytechnic, managers and trade unionists working in Sunderland firms and an industrial chaplain. During the third week, which was concerned with 'The Practical Implications for Ministry', help was given by: clergy working in the following situations – a self-contained parish, a team ministry, a new town and industrial mission. I was present all the time as theological consultant and so of course was the tutor and chairman of the course, who is a lecturer in politics at Sunderland Polytechnic, and a resource that was in use all the time was the skills of the members themselves. The whole operation was sponsored by the Durham Diocesan Further Training for the Clergy and the Durham University Extra-Mural Department. The extra-mural department was responsible for the finances and the premises of the polytechnic were used.

This list gives some indication of the range of experience and skills that must be brought into play, when the church tries to respond to a whole situation. All these skills are needed if theology is to be done in relation to the questions of life, and as part of the search for the meaning in life, and theology itself is the key to the whole process.

The possibilities of theology in this kind of setting are exciting. Instead of being seen as a separate subject theology was integrated into the whole course. Members identified the actual questions that emerged from the situation and then asked what God might be saying in and through what was happening and what their response should be.

This approach revealed a number of further needs. Most members found it difficult to see the relevance of the theology they had learnt at college, and, as I have already mentioned in chapter III there was the difficulty of finding a common language. Most clergy and professional theologians experience this kind of difficulty and it is here that it is particularly useful to have the help of someone who belongs to another discipline. On this occasion the lay chairman was able to help the members face their problem.

An important point about doing theology in this way is that everyone has something to learn as well as something to give.

The lay chairman was able to help members find a common language, but at the same time, he had to gain a new understanding himself of the place of theology in the search for meaning.

The main reason that theology came to life in this situation was that it was directly related to the actual job of the members. A further impetus to action had been given by the recommendations of the Sunderland commission. This made it necessary to relate the discussions to actual decisions about action. For instance, the issue of co-operation was basic to the commission's recommendations, and it was this that urged members forward to make concrete decisions to initiate ecumenical co-operation in sub-areas within Sunderland.

This direct relation of the course to the job led to two further developments. The members recognized that training had to be a continuing thing. For instance, the clergy saw that as they began to work more closely with the other ministers and lay people in their local areas there would be a need to open up thinking of the kind that had taken place during the course with a wider group of people. They also realized that everyone concerned with the actual job must be involved in further training. This meant involving the laity with the clergy.

Some of us had been aware from the start that lay people should be involved as soon as possible, but the clergy had seen some problems. It was therefore only at the end of the clergy course that lay members of their congregations were invited to spend a week-end on a similar programme. This in turn led to joint meetings of clergy and laity. The numbers were quite small, but, apart from Roman Catholics, there was a good ecumenical cross-section.

Because the whole group was now committed to working together, they continued to meet. Their meetings were not just 'talking shops' but occasions when they could report on progress in their own areas, and share the successes and difficulties of the task. It was this attempt at joint action that convinced the members that they needed continuing opportunities to share their concerns and develop their understanding of what the Christian response should be to the life of Sunderland.

This is the kind of ecumenical action that is usually recommended – starting at the local level. The point I want to make in this whole chapter, however, is that the more successful the local response is the more it is doomed to failure, unless it is supported by some overall vision, strategy and systematization of resources. What happened to this particular group forcibly underlines this point.

As soon as the group grasped something of the vision of what mission involved for Christians in Sunderland they saw the need for some kind of systematization. They were equally clear that they had not got the authority or power to create some overall plan and policy. On the other hand, they felt that their experience was valuable and could enable them to make some useful proposals to the church authorities. In this case 'church authorities' meant first of all the C of E Deanery Synod and the Council of Churches of which the rural dean was also chairman.

The rest of the story can be told very briefly – the group prepared proposals for long-term development and training work to be done for clergy and laity ecumenically throughout Sunderland, with specific and limited proposals for a start with a few courses. This was presented to the Deanery Synod and turned down. As a result the group disbanded.

This was a slap in the face for ecumenical relations, of which the Deanery Synod seemed unaware.

In this case the tragedy was not so much that the Deanery Synod turned down the proposals, in fact they may well have been right to do this – what was wrong was that the Synod made no attempt to enter into any further discussions with members of the group in order to set up something better. It seemed that not only were they totally unconcerned about the feelings of the members of the group, but they were blind to their own need for the skills and experience the group had to offer, and to the need for a comprehensive long-term plan.

A number of skills and needs directly related to the churches' task in Sunderland had been identified, but no plans were made for following these up or integrating them in an alternative plan. In fact no alternative plan was proposed.

This is just one example of the waste of resources by the church – and this sort of thing is bound to go on as long as there is no long term planning. The message of this chapter is that there are potentially plenty of resources about, but that they are being squandered or ignored by lack of systematization.

Systematization involves vision, strategy and planning. It must start from a vision that is open to the possibilities of God's Kingdom and to what it means for each one of us to be actively responding to its demands. It must be able to focus on the realities of the present with its specific needs and possibilities, that is, to be clear about where we are as well as what direction we want to take.

This is not the usual activist plea simply to get involved, but it is a plea to systematize the resources that can help us to respond to what God is calling us to in and through the people and events of our own time and to do this in the only way that is open to us – that is in terms of our own situation.

If this reponse is to be made, there must be a strategy for the development of the resources that can enable it to happen. I have shown how varied these resources are and that many of the skills that are needed are those of people who are outside the churches. Such people are more than ready to share in the search and they also want to share the vision that inspires the search. Without this sense of direction and purpose the whole enterprise founders and this is why theology and the development of theologians must be at the heart of the strategy.

I have tried in this book to describe the kind of theological understanding and skills that are needed in an industrial society, and how essential it is for theology to be a joint effort. This is not what is usually expected of theology and people need help in order to develop new understanding and new styles of doing theology.

The purpose of theology and of the theologian is to enable the church to respond to what God is calling it to in the present. Theology has strayed so far from this understanding of itself that we now need to make a major effort to draw out and develop the kind of skills that will enable it to return to this down-to-earth purpose. A main factor in our strategy must be the development of theological resources.

I do not wish to generalize about how this should be done. On the other hand it seems so important to be as specific as possible that I intend to say something about how I am personally involved with others in a planned development of theological resources. I am not setting this out as a blue print, but trying to show the sort of thing that is possible, so that the reader may see some possibilities among which he may choose for himself what is useful in his own situation.

I have already given a number of examples of how theological resources are being developed in the North East. In the last chapter for instance lay groups both inside and outside the church were mentioned, and in this chapter the clergy/lay group in Sunderland has been described. In the Appendix at the end of the book I have brought together brief descriptions of five different types of theology groups in order to show how taken together they represent the beginnings of a strategy for the development of theological resources in the region. Such resources are at least potentially to be found in lay people both outside and inside the churches – in clergy and congregations working together, in the new insights of the sector ministries, in academic theology and in ecumenical dialogue.

In order to draw out what is involved in this kind of development I want to point to some important features of the last two groups.

The first of these groups is concerned with the question of how the contribution of academic theologians can be used in the best way. The academic theologian is essential to theology, but he cannot do theology alone. He needs to be in touch with the raw material of theology which is all that is happening in the world, and as long as he is seen as 'the expert' who does theology for everyone else, he is unable to do theology at all.

It was this problem that the group was set up to tackle and it did this by bringing together a number of academic theologians with an equal number of 'field-working' clergy and lay people. It was considered that everyone had something to learn from everyone else – for the 'field-workers' would be able to see their questions in the perspective of academic theology and the academics would be put in a position where they could give greater weight to the data and questions of everyday life. I have described this in more detail in the Appendix and my purpose here is to show how this group contributes to an overall plan for the development and use of resources.

Academic theologians are specialists in particular aspects of theology, which means that no one academic theologian spans the whole field. In addition they differ profoundly in the position they take in relation to theology in general. Unless one is aware of the fundamental issues that currently divide theologians, every debate can get bogged down before it starts. One reason for this is that the divide in theology centres on what may popularly be called the question of relevance. In theological terms this means that the basic division concerns the relation of man's action in the world to the eternal purposes of God. All through this book I have tried to show that there are polarities in Christian thought that are leading Christians to pull in different directions and that these must be transcended if we are to arrive at a deeper understanding of faith. It is the job of academic theologians to understand these divisions and we need their help if we are to work through them. If this is not understood, the polarities make any continuing dialogue impossible.

There is of course another aspect of the question of relevance. The specialist, simply because he is a specialist tends to be less aware of the questions that must be dealt with in day to day life. It is here that the 'field-working' clergy and the lay people have something to offer, for they must be struggling all the time to relate faith and life, and in the end it is their situation that the academic theologian must help to interpret. Many local ministers lack confidence in their theological ability because they have learnt from experience that the academic theology they learnt at college does not meet the needs of their actual situations. As a result many of them have jettisoned what they learnt academically for a more pragmatic approach, which now needs to be deepened by giving a legitimate but secondary place to academic theology.

The 'field-working' clergy were in fact able to make a significant contribution to this group by their understanding of the views of both the academics and the lay people.

It speaks volumes about the neglect of the development of lay skills to say that it was hard to find lay people who had sufficient theological background to make a full contribution to the group.

The question that lies behind all the other questions that the group tackles is the question about the nature and place of theology. On the whole we have found it most helpful to 'do theology' rather than to talk about it, but from time to time we feel we have gained enough in the way of new insights to come back to this fundamental question. In this way a group of people who are all in their own way skilled theologians, are coming to a shared understanding of the importance of theology and a commitment to theology as a joint enterprise that is vitally important to the whole church.

The group is not an end in itself but a means by which the pursuit of theology is deepened and shared, and relationships between theologians are built up. Even in an unplanned situation this is having a considerable effect beyond the group itself. Many of the members have responsibility in other institutions or groups and members are helping each other in their own sphere of operation, whether these are university, college, church, parish, or unstructured groups. In this way a network of theologians is being created through which the task of theology can be done and through which the members themselves can continue to grow.

What I have said about revelation and theology in chapters II and III will have shown why I consider the work of academic theologians to be so vital. Their work is crucial because they must continually search for the clues that emerge from an understanding of God's word in Christ in the past to the meaning of God's word in Christ today.

The second group I want to describe is an ecumenical group of clergy and lay people. Many of the groups with which I am involved include people of different denominations, but this particular group differs from the others in that it was specifically set up to represent all the main denominations in the North East region.

The North East Ecumenical Group to which I have already referred, agreed to appoint one lay person and one minister each to work on an ecumenical theological study for a period of eighteen months. The object of this was to discover ways in which the ecumenical work that the NEEG aimed to stimulate could be given appropriate theological backing. The resulting group consisted of fourteen members, including representatives of the Church of England (two dioceses), Roman Catholic, Methodist, United Reformed and Baptist Churches and the Salvation Army. At the time of writing the group has almost finished a report that it will discuss with the NEEG. Many of the issues raised are those that have been high-lighted in other contexts in this book. The same divisions cut through the group, and we discovered that these had little or nothing to do with differences of denomination. We did not try to reach a consensus but rather to pursue our differences until we had dug deep enough to discover what was simply a matter of different words and expressions and what was fundamental. Among these differences two seem especially important – the first is the division between those who believe the church must have a clear message that is based on factual certainties, and those who are aware of the mystery of life and of God and the difficulty of making any definitive statements. The second division concerns the place of the church in Christian life and thinking. These divisions seem particularly important as they touch on the practicalities of how theology is done and how mission is effected.

We have no answer to offer in these matters and indeed the burden of the group's report is that all that it has been able to do is open up questions which now need further study in order that the differences may be transcended.

The fact that members of the group were appointed by their churches rather than coming together as a group of like-minded people meant that a whole spectrum of theological outlooks was represented. This added to a difficulty that every group experiences in settling down and doing any joint work at all. There was a moment when it seemed that this would never happen and that the group would split up. It was, I believe, only the fact that the members had been asked by their churches to do a specific and limited job that got the group over this hump. Even in a group that had been appointed for the purpose of doing theology, there were considerable reservations about the worthwhileness of any kind of theology. This is understandable in the light of what I have said about the commonly held view that theology and life are separate.

The achievement of the group consisted in facing this sort of problem and emerging with the feeling that they had been enriched by the experience and had positive proposals for further ecumenical study.

These two groups with the other groups mentioned in the Appendix are pilot schemes, which simply aim to explore potential theological resources and ways of developing them. The need now is to make use of what has been learnt in order to systematize the development and use of all resources in the region.

The kind of systematization for which I have been pleading in this chapter would involve the following steps:

1. Developing a cadre of people who can help others 'do theology' as a joint enterprise. This means spending time helping a small number of people develop their own skills before trying to increase the number of groups.

2. Building up a register of people with specific skills or disciplines, who would be willing to share these during a weekend or a series of evenings each year. These people would include for instance, sociologists, behavioural scientists, political scientists, economists, etc. It would be necessary to spend some time helping them to share the vision and aims of the whole plan and discovering whether they could work in unstructured situations.

3. Analysing the different needs to be met. For instance, I have mentioned six different areas of lay responsibility.[1]

4. Meeting the different needs in different ways. For instance three of the areas of lay responsibility can be dealt with at a comparatively local level, but the others need to bring people together from a wider area.

5. Deploying resources where they are wanted – so that resources go to the point of need rather than being concentrated at some central place.

6. This means that the organization aimed at is a network of

relationships among all sorts of people and that its coherence derives from a shared vision, and does not depend upon some central building or institute. The aim is to create situations in which everyone can learn from everyone else. The organization is therefore more like the Open University than any other institution.

7. Continuing a programme of identifying new resources and developing skills.

8. Continuing research, especially of the theological kind I have mentioned in relation to some of the groups and in an analysis of the changing questions of life in the North East.

9. Only a limited number of full-time staff would be needed. These should include a director, a theological consultant and an administrator.

10. A management board made up of a majority of lay people involved in different aspects of the region's life would oversee the policy and programme.

11. It would be ecumenically sponsored.[2]

How can this process be started, and what immediate steps towards systematization can be taken?

The first step for anyone who sees the point of doing this must be a step towards ecumenical co-operation. In this region we are fortunate to have the North East Ecumenical Group. If there is no group in your area perhaps you should do something about it. The existence of this group is one safeguard against individual denominations doing things on their own that might be better done together, and makes it possible for common understandings of needs and policies to develop.

But do not expect too much from this kind of group. The denominations are far stronger than any ecumenical structure, and each member of any ecumenical group is under particular constraints from his own denomination.

The amalgamation of the different denominational training departments is definitely not the answer! The result of premature attempts to amalgamate structures could be more committees rather than more work on the ground. What should be possible is some sharing of resources on specific projects rather than duplicating everything.

What does seem to be important is that there should be shared thinking about what the needs are so that whatever policies are developed will be the result of shared thinking – rather than someone hatching up an idea and then suggesting others join in.

Exactly the same point must be made about clergy/lay co-operation. Lay people must be involved in deciding what the questions are as well as in how they should be tackled. If this point is taken seriously it really will revolutionize our structures.

The crucial point that must be kept in mind all the time is that resources for doing theology will only be developed by actually doing theology. That is where change must start – by some people doing just that.

NOTES

1. See above p. 107.
2. Something of this kind has been proposed in the Teesside 'Christian Urban Exploration' Scheme. This proposal for a training and research unit grew out of the needs emerging from a great deal of experimental work that has been going on in Teesside for a number of years. The proposal was accepted by the church leaders concerned and by the Teesside Council of Churches in 1970, but so far the unit has not been set up.

XI

GOING ON FROM WHERE WE ARE

We began by listening to a conversation between four men who work in industry. Recently I have had the chance of catching up with the affairs of Bob, John, Jonathan and Fergus.

There continue to be changes in the local management in Bob's firm, but Bob has managed to reach a deeper level of trust and understanding with the managing director of the parent company. In one of their conversations recently this director told Bob that, at the time of the redundancies, it had been the intention of the directors to close the Hartlepool branch and that this had only been prevented by the action of the men. Now, far from closing down, things look quite bright for the future.

Bob emphasized how important his relationship with the industrial chaplain had been, saying: 'He was the only person I could talk openly to about all this, and he gave me the encouragement to go on in spite of all the difficulties.'

This is not to say that Bob has no problems. As a member of the AEUW District Committee he is involved with questions that affect engineering workers throughout the country; and as a district councillor he is helping to steer the Hartlepool Borough Council through the first stages of its incorporation in the new Cleveland County.

There have been changes in John's situation too, for he has been promoted to a larger plant. This says something about his achievements in keeping production up during a difficult period in his previous position. But it means he will now be in a position of even greater pressure. During the last few weeks steel workers in Teesside had another shock when it was announced that, owing to a shortage of raw materials, there would be a cut-back in production. At the same time there have been a number of changes in senior management, which suggests that the pressure upon managers to improve performance will be increased. These pressures are not generated locally, but reflect changes throughout the world – and not least in the European Community. They point to the inter-dependence of the steel industry and its place in this country as a barometer of the changing position of Britain in the world economy.

Jonathan and Fergus are both still working at the Consett Iron Works of the British Steel Corporation. It is only people who know something of their performance at work, who can understand that their continuing confidence in their situation is based on their ability to achieve very high standards of steel making while adapting to the new techniques and greater speeds that are required today. The combined skills of these two men, and the kind of team work that it takes to produce good steel is beyond the comprehension of the average 'layman'. They are facing technical change but between them they have been able to cope with it.

These are just four men who are in situations where life puts questions against their humanity. It is at points like this that the search for meaning in life and in faith is most sharply focussed.

The question we have to answer is therefore 'What resources do men and women have and what resources might they have for living hopefully and creatively with these questions?' On any Christian assumption *theology* is relevant to this question, because theology is about God and about what he has done and what he will do for us. It is for this reason that this book is about theology in an industrial society. There can be no task that is more pressing than that of 'doing theology' in an industrial society. If the church does not get to grips with this question as a matter of urgency it will be letting down the people who face the real questions of meaning in life today, and at the same time it will be turning its back on God.

It is easy to feel that the job is impossible, that nothing can be changed and that the pressures of large institutions, the momentum of events and habitual ways of thinking cannot be influenced. But the resources that are there – in any situation – are immense.

No wonder we get dejected if we start from the wrong end, and wait for the 'system' or some 'expert' to answer our need. The questions must be faced where we are, and it is here that we must look for resources. 'Doing theology' means trying to discern God *in* the situation, and it means receiving from him the resources that are at hand – and this means first and foremost, people – for 'doing theology' is a corporate thing. In Bob's case, he found one friend with whom he could share his questions.

As it happened this friend was an industrial chaplain, but it might well have been one of his work mates.

'Doing theology' in this instance was a matter of the chaplain being alongside Bob so that together they could explore the question of meaning and of faith. The chaplain certainly did not say very much, for his role was largely that of listener. But it is in this kind of exchange that God offers us his Spirit and that we gain encouragement to make creative response. The 'Go-between-God' is J. V. Taylor's description of the Holy Spirit and this catches the truth that things we do not anticipate begin to happen when people come together with a real concern for each other.

To take another example – the pressure upon John to accept the general understandings of meaning that are at work in his immediate situation are so great that it is difficult for him to stand outside them in an objective way. He found the resources he needed in membership of a group that included managers and trade unionists from a number of different companies in the area. Meeting with people who had similar experiences, but in different situations, gave him the freedom he needed in order to understand his own situation in new ways.

We should not feel hopeless and dejected – but should expect to find resources where we are for these are the resources that God gives. We should encourage each other to respond creatively and so to discover God himself as he calls us into life.

St Paul points to the fact that the whole creation is involved in the agonizing process of new birth: 'The whole creation has been groaning in travail together until now' (Rom. 8.22). In this process it is the Spirit of God that is the liberating force so that in the end the creation itself 'will be set free from its bondage to decay and obtain the glorious liberty of the children of God' (Rom. 8.21). This passage in Romans makes it absolutely clear that nothing is outside God's activity and that our own responses only find meaning within God's purpose for the whole world. In this context discipleship means going on from where we are in order to share in this process. This can be a very hopeful and challenging thing.

The goal of the whole process is the Kingdom of God – which 'stands for the fulfilment of the personal purposes of the universe in a perfected and a perfecting society'.[1] Too often in our anxieties about the church we seem to have forgotten that it was the Kingdom of God that was the centre of Jesus' concern. The miracles he performed were signs of the present reality of the

Kingdom. The parables he told pointed to ways in which the Kingdom was actually taking shape as people responded to life in different situations. In the story of the sheep and the goats (Matt. 25.31 ff.) the point is driven home that creative and concerned response to people and to life contributes to the Kingdom whether it is done by those who do or do not know him by name. In this light the issue of discipleship and what it means is acutely raised.

A concern for the Kingdom forces us out into life to put ourselves at the disposal of God there, and the call to discipleship is a call to respond to the actualities of our own particular situation. This brings us back to a consideration of the unique value of each person. The Jews missed the whole point by thinking that God's call conferred status and privilege, making them better than anyone else. What God's call points to, however, is the uniqueness of *every* nation and of *every* person. In the Bible this uniqueness is recognized by the giving of a name – for instance of the pagan king Cyrus the prophet says: 'Thus says the Lord ... I call you by your name, I surname you, though you do not know me' (Isa. 45.1, 4).

The Kingdom of God is a mystery (Mark 4.11) just because it is the Kingdom of *God*. Our understanding is always partial, but we must struggle to discern what we can of it so that we may be released from our anxieties and go forward in expectation and hope.

Discipleship means being on the move – and that means that we must discover our fellowship, study and prayer wherever we are. John, for instance, found the fellowship he needed in the managers' and trade unionists' group. Within this group and using their resources he was able to think through his own questions. It was only when these resources had been pushed as far as possible that outside people were brought in. Then a university lecturer in industrial affairs helped the group see what might be the consequences for them of Britain's entry to the European Community, and an industrial chaplain helped them to 'do theology' by exploring some main themes of Christian faith – justice, creativity and suffering – in relation to their industrial situations. Prayer is today a problem for Christian and non-Christian alike, and I cannot do better than quote advice given by Mark Gibbard. 'First I would encourage enquirers to go on meeting people, to try to understand them more deeply and to help them more effectively.... Secondly, I would recommend to them a way of reflecting on and exploring into life. This could be a kind of meditating ...'[2] This is advice for a start and it seems to me that what we have said about 'doing theology' is also a lead into this kind of praying.

What I am concerned with here is to make clear that Christian discipleship is about responding to God's call to go forward from where we are extending into life. This is an exciting and often stressful thing, and it is the layman who faces the greatest demands. The church's role is to give what help and inspiration it can in this task. Rather than encouraging, however, the church often inhibits freedom of response.

Many who may be called to make a particular contribution to the Kingdom are made to feel guilty about their relationship with the rest of the church. One church member, for instance, became very active in his trade union. The union meetings were held at the same time as the church service on Sunday mornings, and, as this was a small mining community, church members would see him going to the union meetings as they were going to church. Far from leading to an understanding of his particular calling this led to the church members refusing to speak to him.

Tensions are allowed to build up between those who are engaged in the maintenance of the established work of the churches and those who are working on the frontiers opening up new areas of work. For instance industrial chaplains are often made to feel that they are out on a limb as church members continue to ask what contribution they are making to the church. The unfortunate result of this continued pressure is that instead of facing the really difficult questions of industrial life they spend their energies trying to convince the rest of the church that they are 'loyal' members of the institution.

This all points to the fact that we have confused the church with the Kingdom. Of course it is absolutely essential that there is a church. Its function is to keep alive in the world the vision of the Kingdom and in its own life to represent the qualities and relationships of the Kingdom. This means that the church must be a community in which members give support to each other and in which love and trust make it possible to have a rich diversity within its unity. The church's concern should not be to draw people into its own orbit, but to help them respond to their calling in the world. This means providing the necessary resources, and I have shown that above all this means producing people who can help others 'do theology' at the actual points of disturbance and questioning. The church must not be afraid of 'doing theology' for it is the means by which people are helped to discover the resources of God so that they can live creatively with these questions.

When lay people push their own resources and those they find in their immediate situations as far as they can, they must then demand of the church whatever else they require. This will be a novel and refreshing situation for it will no longer be a case of the clergy stirring up the laity, but the laity stirring up the clergy. And the clergy must respond for they are mandated to work as much with those who are outside the church as with those who are inside.

Those who have resisted the idea of the church's involvement in the world have rightly seen that this must lead to conflict. We do not have to go any further than Bob and his managing director to see that in any one situation two people may decide to respond in different ways. But what could possibly lead us to imagine that we can avoid the cross?

In addition to losing the cosmic dimension of the Kingdom we seem to have lost any sense of the toughness and struggle of it all. We have for instance, no idea of the depths of what is referred to as 'sufferings', 'glory', 'groaning', 'intercession', bondage', 'liberty' in the Epistle to the Romans (Rom. 8.18-27).

This is why we must get theology going at the actual points where suffering and struggle are most intense – 'the aloneness of the people in the technology of a modern hospital, the terror of a child with a suspected fractured skull at the mercy of a radiologist carrying out a routine, the destroying boredom even more than the violence of a blackboard jungle, the lostness of the aged who are marginalised and condescended to ...'[3] and much more that we close our eyes to in our industrial society. If we really considered some of these things in relation to what the Bible is saying, the words would cry out to us with new meaning and we might begin to know also what is meant by 'sin' and 'grace', 'heaven' and 'hell'. Of course we all know something about suffering and stress in our own experience but too often we fail to recognize God the disturber in it.

The very stuff of creativity is stressful and demanding, and love, far from being a soft, accommodating thing, is a very tough commodity.

The reality and the depths of struggle in life show that Mission 'A' is right to try to preserve the apocalyptic elements in Christian faith, but wrong to isolate its meaning from present events.

We should not be afraid of our differences for it is only through the opposition of ideas and attitudes that new levels of under-

standing can be reached. The exploration of meaning must often
be in and through conflict. In this book I am not producing a
manual for appropriate modern theology in easy stages, but pointing to a mystery that no one can understand. I have shown that
neither the view of Mission 'A' or Mission 'B', when pushed to
their extremes, is satisfactory. For when it comes to 'doing
theology' Mission 'A' talks about God, but is unable to show
what this means for daily living; while Mission 'B' is not really
concerned with theology at all, feels unable to mention God in
any way that can convey meaning and thinks it is enough simply
to be involved.

It may seem that I too am saying 'Forget about God', because
I am stressing the action that must take place in the world, at
the points where disturbance is greatest and where meaning is
under question. It may seem that I am suggesting that 'doing
theology' is no more than listening and encouraging, but this is
not true – for the whole burden of what I am saying throughout
this book is 'Look for God in and through the disturbances of
life'.

'The Spirit (wind) blows where it wills ...' (John 3.8) and it
can be 'like the rush of a mighty wind' (Acts 2.2). We are certainly
far from being able to calculate his movements, but to commit
ourselves to his leading can be exciting and glorious. The Spirit
stirs things up and it is never possible to get things back where
they were. Our response does contribute to change though the
results are seldom what we intended. The most lasting contribution we make to any situation is the spirit in which we shared
in it – so that in some way we ourselves become part of life
instead of being apart from it.

This openness to the Spirit catches the true meaning of
spirituality – and this leads me to the last polarity that I want
to mention. Too often the spirituality we are offered is not a
spirituality of life but of escape from life.

In this book I have been urging the need to transcend these
polarities by struggling to find a deeper understanding of life
and of faith. Our problem is that life and faith have been unnaturally separated, so that the majority of Christians think in
terms of two realities instead of one.

But Christian faith is about the one reality that is in Christ:
'Sharing in Christ we stand at once both in the reality of God
and the reality of the world.... The New Testament is concerned
solely with the manner in which the reality of Christ assumes
reality in the present world, which it has already encompassed,
seized and possessed.... The unity of the reality of God and of

the world which has been accomplished in Christ, is repeated, or, more exactly, is realized, ever afresh in the life of man.'[4]

Therefore, our only hope of finding meaning in life and in faith is to struggle to understand the meaning of Christ. I am convinced by my own experience that many people want to take part in this search. I am also convinced that there are ample resources for 'doing theology' even though some of them are in deep freeze. In putting immense questions against our humanity, our industrial society puts even bigger questions against our faith so that we are faced with the urgency of pressing the questions Bonhoeffer asked: 'What is Christianity and indeed what is Christ for us today?' This question demands that we release all the energies and resources we can for 'doing theology' in and for our industrial society.

NOTES

1. David Jenkins, *The Glory of Man*, SCM Press 1967, p. 116.
2. Mark Gibbard, *Why Pray?*, SCM Press 1970, p. 14.
3. David Jenkins, *Innovation and the Response to Mystery*, an unpublished paper.
4. Dietrich Bonhoeffer, *Ethics*, SCM Press 1955, pp. 170-1.

APPENDIX

Some Examples of 'Doing Theology'

Should be read with Chapter III

The five following examples illustrate how theology can be a joint enterprise. These are all groups with which I am working. I have not, however, seen them as five separate entities, but as parts of an overall plan to identify and develop theological resources, and to use these resources and all that we discover together to stimulate this kind of theological work throughout the region. In this way resources will be developed that can enable the whole church to make some impact upon the whole region.

These groups can only be developed, where real theological exploration is actually going on, on the ground in all sorts of informal ways, including very secular situations where theology is done only in a secular manner. It is only out of this ongoing open dialogue about life's questions that people emerge who wish to engage in more formal theological discussion.

(a) A LAY GROUP FROM INDUSTRY

Membership The group developed out of the work of industrial mission. A number of men who were more or less remote from the church came to see that Christian faith might have some relevance to their lives as a result of the work of industrial chaplains. Following a consultation arranged by the industrial mission some of them embarked on a regular theological study planned round their own questions.

Aims The group aims to gain a fresh understanding of Christian faith by starting from issues and questions that the members perceive in their own lives in industry.

Organization Meetings are held monthly on Sunday mornings and are sponsored by the Durham University Extra-Mural Department. A professional theologian serves the group, not as lecturer but as consultant. With various changes of membership the group has continued with attendances of 10-20 since 1965. A residential week-end usually takes place each year. The group now includes some who are not engaged in industry, notably the wives of some of the original members.

Content The members' own questions form the starting point: 'In industry there always seems to be a tension between efficiency and human welfare. What has the Christian doctrine of man to say to this?' 'What is the relation between the church's ministry of forgiveness and action in situations where all the alternatives are less than satisfactory?', etc. A general outline planned by the whole group is submitted to the extra-mural department for each session. This may be as general as *social ethics* or *towards a twentieth century theology*.

Method An open participative style is adopted in which it is recognized that no holds are barred and no belief is too sacred to question. At the same time there is a good deal of group work and members prepare introductions and case studies from their own situations. The consultant theologian's role is to challenge assumptions, to see that there is a proper discipline in sticking to the point and the use of language, and to introduce information relevant to the question under discussion. This must include contemporary experience and knowledge (A in the diagram) and material from the Bible and Christian traditions (B in the diagram). A box containing books for borrowing is always well used.

Outcome The first outcome is felt in the members' own lives. They began by asking about the relevance of Christian faith to life in industry, and it is in their lives in industry that the first gain is felt. Of course, it does not stop there but helps towards unification of their whole lives.

The second result is that lay people are gaining an intelligent understanding of their faith and an ability to articulate this in a relevant way. They can therefore make a vital contribution to the church's own understanding of itself and its impact on the world. Members of the group are being used to help other groups both inside and outside the church. Unfortunately, the church does not yet seem able to use lay people effectively.

This group shows that there are lay people who, given the opportunity to do theology in a sustained and disciplined way, can make a vital contribution to both church and world today.

(*b*) AN ECUMENICAL GROUP OF CLERGY AND LAITY

Membership I felt the need to work with a group that was fully representative of the major denominations in the region and asked the North East Ecumenical Group of church leaders to appoint one minister and one layman from each denomination to work with me on a pilot theological project for a period of eighteen months. The group has fourteen members which include: four Anglicans (two each from the Dioceses of Durham and Newcastle), two Roman Catholics, one Methodist (the layman was unable to continue as he is working overseas for a time), two from the United Reformed Church, two Baptists, two Salvation Army members and myself.

Aims The aim is to share insights and problems of communicating the gospel: to reach understanding, (not consensus) across different ways of expressing Christian faith, identifying any major differences of approach and noting whether these are personal or denominational: to discover how a group like this can do theology together: to write up any conclusions about content and method that might be helpful to further ecumenical co-operation in presenting the gospel in the North East.

Organization Meetings are held on the last Friday of each month from 6.00 to 9.30 p.m. They are held in Durham as the most central point and begin with a buffet meal. Donations from the sponsoring churches cover the cost of the room, food and postage for the circulation of working papers, which may be the work of individuals or summaries of group work. The life of the group is limited to eighteen months by which time we should present a report to the North East Ecumenical Group.

Content The group decided to limit its considerations to 'Overcoming the Credibility Gap' and to prepare a report that would give some analysis of the nature of the credibility gap and how it might be overcome. In order to do this they have concentrated on the positive aspects of faith and each member has given some account of the faith he personally lives by. We have then tried to identify points at which there are real differences. The purpose of this is not to try to reach agreement but to appreciate something of the richness of the various Christian traditions.

Method The first few months were very difficult and nothing seemed to work. We tried working in two groups but there was a good deal of dissatisfaction with the process. There were obviously widely different points of view in the group but there was a low level of communication about the real issues. After a few months this came into the open and after discussing it we settled down to a deeper level of commitment, acceptance and honesty with each other. Later each member wrote a personal statement of 'The faith I live by', which was circulated to all the other members. At the following meeting each member paired with the person he 'least understood' in order to examine points of agreement and disagreement and questions that needed more attention. We do not think we should try to reconcile differences but see that they are creative in keeping the tension we live in until the final Kingdom. Minutes are circulated between meetings and the main conclusions are being brought together to form a short report.

Outcome The outcome will not be any sort of agreed statement of faith. There will be a short report to the NEEG which will say how the group sees the mission needs of the region, shows that the churches must take account of different approaches – even though these are not primarily denominational – and the need for ecumenical action to be backed up by continuing ecumenical theological work. The report will also say that this kind of exploration is a painful and slow process and something about the conditions which are necessary for any success.

This group shows that ecumenical action needs the support of ecumenical theological work: that it is possible and helpful for people with different points of view to work together provided they commit themselves to a long and painful process.

(*c*) A GROUP OF ACADEMIC AND 'FIELD-WORKING' THEOLOGIANS

Membership The original members were invited in order to make a total of sixteen in which there were equal numbers of academic and 'field-working' theologians. The term 'field-worker' was used to emphasize the fact that it is not only academics who should be called theologians, but that the term properly includes clergy in the 'field', in both parochial and other ministry, and lay people. As well as aiming at the academic/field-working mixture, this group was chosen to represent an ecumenical cross-section of people throughout the North East region. Inevitably membership has changed during the four years of the group's life and although the group is still roughly representative of those it aimed to include, the most constant members have been the 'field-working' clergy.

Aims The aim was to enable a joint theological exploration to take place in which the work of academic theologians and of 'field-working' theologians could contribute to the development of a theology that relates faith and life. It was considered that all members would gain from working together. 'Field-workers' would be able to see their questions in the perspective of academic disciplines, while academic theologians would have the opportunity of giving greater weight to the theological data of daily life.

Organization About six meetings take place at intervals throughout the academic year. Meetings are held in Durham as the most central place in the region.

Content At alternate meetings the group starts from a practical situation in order to discover in discussion what theological points may be relevant to it, and from a Christian doctrine in order to discover whether it has practical implications for daily living. From time to time a whole meeting is spent discussing the implications of what we have done for an understanding of the nature of theology and how it should be done. We have however tried to concentrate on actually doing theology rather than talking about theology.

Method The topics have usually been introduced by the members themselves. We have only asked people from outside when we have not got the necessary experience within the group itself. For instance, no one in the group carries political responsibility, so on two occasions we have invited people with this experience to open up.

Outcome This has opened up a very useful dialogue with academic theologians. This dialogue is partly being continued outside the group, for on the whole the academic theologians have been less committed to the group than other members. The strength of the group has in fact been in the 'field-working' clergy, for we have only found a few lay people who have sufficient theological background to join fully in this project.

There are deep divisions within the group, and these relate in various ways to the question of 'relevance'. Behind the differences that arise from different professional concerns – the academic for 'pure' theology versus the 'field-worker' for practical implications – there is a fundamental difference about the way we understand God's relation to the world. This needs to be opened up at a deeper theological level if progress is to be made.

This group shows that the work of academic theologians is essential to the whole theological task and that specific steps must be taken to relate their work to that of 'field-working' theologians.

(*d*) A COURSE FOR CLERGY AND LAY PEOPLE ON URBAN MINISTRY (The Sunderland Course)

Membership This course proceeded in two stages:
(i) for clergy only, and (ii) for lay people from their congregations and from the Sunderland Council of Churches Executive Committee. Clergy working in Sunderland of all denominations were invited with the proviso that they must attend the whole course. Twelve clergy enrolled – ten Church of England, including the rural dean, one Methodist and one United Reformed Church.

Aims To help clergy gain a theological understanding of the nature of urban/industrial society and its specific questions, and to see its implications for the church's ministry. The immediate impetus behind the course was the general acceptance of a policy of working towards the whole church in Sunderland working as a team in relation to the whole town – and the belief that this needed educational back-up.

Organization The course was sponsored by the Durham Extra-Mural Department in consultation with the Durham Diocesan Further Training of the Clergy, and the Sunderland Council of Churches. The extra-mural department appointed a course tutor who is a lecturer in politics at Sunderland Polytechnic and a theological consultant was also present throughout the course. The course was non-residential and was held at Sunderland Polytechnic. The course consisted of three separate weeks spaced throughout one year.

Content and Method Lectures on Sunderland's life and some of the underlying sociological issues involved. Discussion with people engaged in specific aspects of the town's life. Discussion with ministers having 'sector' experience. Lectures on the main theological issues involved in a ministry to society. Discussion of theological issues and the implications of the course for ministry.

Week 1 Civic and community life with special emphasis on the family.

Week 2 Industrial life.

Week 3 Implications for ministry.

Discussion among the members themselves in groups formed the most important part of the course. What was crucial was the way the tutor drew together their considerations and helped them to make decisions about what this meant for action.

Outcome (i) Decisions were made by the members to try to develop ecumenical co-operation between congregations in their own local areas and work is going ahead in this respect.

(ii) It was decided to hold a week-end for lay people from the same congregations represented by the clergy on the course so that they might share some of the insights they had gained.

(iii) The result of this week-end was that clergy and laity continued to work together on local ecumenical co-operation and on plans for a continuing ecumenical training and development programme.

This group shows that theology needs to be done in relation to the actual job: that all the people concerned in the job (clergy and laity) need to be involved: that a continuing programme of training and development is needed if the job is to progress.

(*e*) SECTOR MINISTERS' DEVELOPMENT – a group of industrial chaplains

Membership Industrial chaplains of the Northumberland and North Durham Industrial Mission.

Aims To help them develop the kind of theological understanding and skills needed in their ministry.

Organization Discussion among the chaplains about their ministry and the training needs they themselves had recognized. Plans to meet these needs made by a sub-group including the theological consultant.

Content The following needs were identified: skills in identifying and developing theological issues in secular situations, to know what others had actually been able to achieve in similar situations, behavioural and group discussion skills, to explicate the meaning of – 'God is at work in the world'. These needs formed the basis of the programme.

Method Lay people were needed to describe what had actually been achieved in similar situations. This led to a Sunday afternoon and evening meeting with four laymen from various theology groups so that they could share their experience with the chaplains in the context of the overall aims of industrial mission. Following this one of the laymen gave two Sunday afternoons to trainings in discussion group work. The behavioural needs are being met by the chaplains attending training courses sponsored by Durham University Business School. The more specific theological question of God's activity in the world is now being tackled by a series of overnight consultations involving chaplains from both industrial mission teams and with the help of an outside theological consultant.

Outcome Theological training needs to take place in relation to the needs of the job, and plans must be made in full consultation with the members themselves. General courses that are laid on from above cannot meet the actual needs and fail to gain commitment. A number of different resources are needed and where lay resources are involved timing must be arranged to suit the laymen. Although this kind of training is being explored by industrial chaplains it is relevant to the whole church and particularly to other forms of sector ministry.

This group shows that the people concerned must help to plan their own training and development in relation to their own perceived needs.